The WALL
between
CHURCH
and
STATE

EDITOR

DALLIN H. OAKS

CONTRIBUTORS

ROBERT F. DRINAN

HAROLD E. FEY

MURRAY A. GORDON

WILLIAM GORMAN

ROBERT M. HUTCHINS

PAUL G. KAUPER

PHILIP B. KURLAND

MONRAD G. PAULSEN

The WALL

between

CHURCH

and

STATE

THE UNIVERSITY OF CHICAGO PRESS

CHICAGO AND LONDON

Library of Congress Catalog Card Number: 63-20897

THE UNIVERSITY OF CHICAGO PRESS, CHICAGO & LONDON
The University of Toronto Press, Toronto 5, Canada

DALLIN H. OAKS

ROBERT M. HUTCHINS

HAROLD E. FEY

WILLIAM GORMAN

ROBERT F. DRINAN

MURRAY A. GORDON

PAUL G. KAUPER

MONRAD G. PAULSEN

PHILIP B. KURLAND

Contents

Introduction

Problems of the relationship between church and state bedevil this generation. Their solution is complicated by the difficulties inherent in reasoning upon and communicating about matters that touch the innermost fabric of belief, religious or irreligious. But an acceptable and enduring solution of such problems will not be found without reason nor accepted without effective communication. The quest for reason must explore the breadth and depth of church-state relationships in this country, unencumbered by irrational individual predilections. Those who would aid in the search should be willing to reconsider preconceived notions of right, wisdom, and law. Then, if there is to be communication about the problems and solutions, opposing factions must talk with one another, not at one another.[1] There must be a greater exchange of views. Too much of what is written about church-state problems is circulated by media identified with one position or another to readers already committed to the views espoused. We need more dialogue, less diatribe.

To provide a forum for such a dialogue and to contribute to its students' understanding of representative church-state problems of deep concern to the courts and to the public, the Law School of the University of Chicago recently sponsored a Conference on Church and State. The Conference program was arranged and conducted by a faculty committee composed of Philip B. Kurland, Chairman,

[1] Cogley, *Foreword*, RELIGION AND AMERICAN SOCIETY 6 (Center for the Study of Democratic Institutions 1961).

1

Walter J. Blum, Harry Kalven, Jr., and Dallin H. Oaks. The chapters of this book were prepared as contributions to that Conference
or in response to it.

The Wall

Borrowing Thomas Jefferson's metaphor, Mr. Justice Black's opinions for the Court in the *Everson* and *McCollum* cases speak reso-
lutely of "a wall between Church and State which must be kept high
and impregnable."[2] This striking metaphor, with its comforting con-
notations of certainty and security, now seems to occupy a central—
for some even a dominant—position in the dialogue on church and
state.[3] A discussion of the relationships between church and state
should at least take note of its presence before exploring the en-
virons.

Along the border between church and state "the wall" is not new,
nor is it one-sided. Those who attack the wall in this generation may
appear from the same quarter as those said to have erected it in an
earlier time. Thus, in his address to the nobility, Martin Luther
accused "The Romanists" with having "drawn three walls round
themselves, with which they have hitherto protected themselves, so
that no one could reform them. . . ."[4] The first of these walls was said
to be an artificial separation between a spiritual estate of "Pope,
bishops, priests, and monks," and a temporal estate of "princes,
lords, artificers and peasants."[5]

The modern popularity of the wall metaphor should not conceal
its inappropriateness as an expression of current church-state relationships. Certainly there is something anomalous about a wall that

[2] McCollum v. Board of Education, 333 U.S. 203, 212 (1948) ; Everson v.
Board of Education, 330 U.S. 1, 16, 18 (1947).

[3] *E.g.*, McCollum v. Board of Education, 333 U.S. 203, 213 (1948) (opinion
of Frankfurter, J.) : "We cannot illuminatingly apply the 'wall-of-separation'
metaphor until we have considered. . . ."

[4] Luther, *To the Christian Nobility of the German Nation Respecting the
Reformation of the Christian Estate*, in Luther's Primary Works 162–63
(Wace & Buchheim ed. 1896).

[5] *Id.* at 163–64.

will admit a school bus without the "slightest breach,"[6] but is impermeable to a prayer.[7] Indeed, the metaphor may have its highest and best use as the title of a book.

One need not agree with all that is said by those who deny the existence of a "wall between church and state" in order to join them in the hope that the wall will soon give way to more accurate, if less conclusive, means of describing the relationship between church and state. The metaphor is not an aid to thought and it can be a positive barrier to communication. The needed dialogue will be furthered if the strict separationists come out from behind the wall to discuss their reasons. It will also be facilitated if those who assail the wall will not assume that they can establish their position by demolishing a metaphor.

"The Future of the Wall" is the subject to which Robert M. Hutchins addresses himself in the first chapter. The trumpets are sounding, and Jericho is besieged.

PROBLEMS OF CHURCH AND STATE

SCHOOLS

The First Amendment provision, "Congress shall make no law respecting an establishment of religion, or prohibiting the free exercise thereof," has two parallel participial phrases, usually incorrectly called clauses. Some students of the religion clause have suggested that the free-exercise or "freedom" phrase was the dominant one, to which the "establishment" proscription must give way in the event of conflict. Others might argue the converse: that the paramount aim was to avoid an establishment of religion and that the second phrase was simply a corollary statement of one of the objectives served by the overriding requirement. The tendency to designate one part of the religion clause as primary and the other as secondary seems to grow out of an effort to resolve concrete problems where the nonestablishment and free-exercise requirements seem to be in conflict. Another means of reconciliation is to read the two phrases together as a single precept. According to one authority this approach yields

[6] Everson v. Board of Education, 330 U.S. 1, 18 (1947).

[7] Engel v. Vitale, 370 U.S. 421 (1962).

the command that government make no classification in terms of religion.[8]

In contemporary discussion of the various theories and arguments about the meaning of the First Amendment it is possible to detect a marked tendency to begin with a conclusion about the desirability of one or another solution to some problem and to accept or reject available theories and arguments on the basis of conformity or lack of conformity with that conclusion. The nature of the issues makes this form of "reasoning" understandable, and probably none can claim complete immunity from it. But so confessing does not restore the opportunities for objective inquiry and provocative communication lost by those who engage in this sort of selective inquiry and argumentation.

Only the most narrow separationist would contend that religion, which played such a major role in the establishment of this country and which occupies such an important place in the actions and thinking of so many of its citizens, should not have an honorable place in our public life. In no area of public life is the attainment of an honored status for religion more necessary, or more hazardous, than in our public schools, where knowledge of, and respect for, our societal institutions must be taught. But it is difficult, perhaps impossible, to convey information about religion without the purpose or effect of shaping denominational attitudes and inculcating belief, and the younger the pupil, the greater the risk.

For some, the evident dangers in the subject of religion in the curriculum are so great that they would abolish all mention of God or religion in the public schools, or at least relegate the subject to a brief, non-controversial treatment that would assure its impotence. But the public schools must not, by studiously disregarding or ignoring religion, expressly or impliedly teach irreligion, for irreligion, no less than its denominational antitheses, is capable of being established. As Professor Wilber G. Katz observed recently, the complete elimination of religion from the curriculum of a school that is seeking to teach moral values amounts to an establishment of secu-

---

[8] Kurland, Religion and the Law 18, 112 (1962).

lar humanism.[9] In recent years there have been repeated reminders that irreligion demands the protection of the free-exercise phrase; the irreligious must be equally willing to accept the proscriptions of non-establishment.

The major church-state issue today is the desirability and constitutionality of governmental aid to private, and particularly parochial, schools. On this issue it is normally helpful if these two questions—desirability and constitutionality—are kept separate. The first is a question of legislative and public policy on which every citizen can and should ultimately express his preference. The second is a matter for judicial and other informed opinion. While a judgment on the issue of constitutionality may be affected by the expert's view of its desirability, the two need not coincide. Thus, conscientious lawyers who deem aid desirable may nevertheless think it unconstitutional, and vice versa.

The desirable-undesirable dichotomy at the policy level should not lead one to suppose that there are only two possible views on the issue of constitutionality. There are three. The Constitution (1) prevents aid, (2) permits aid, or (3) requires aid. In considering the arguments of constitutional experts one should determine which of these three views is being espoused. Because of the tendency to confuse the separate issues of policy and legality, one should also determine whether the arguments being mustered are addressed to the question of conformity or non-conformity with the relevant constitutional standards or are, in reality, simply arguments about the desirability or undesirability of the proposed program.

The actual or proposed aid to parochial schools that has occupied public attention during the last few decades originated with the states or their local instrumentalities, such as counties or school districts. At this level the provisions of two constitutions must be considered: the First Amendment of the federal constitution and the comparable provisions of the relevant state constitution. Virtually every state constitution has specific provisions that on their face are more restrictive of state support of religious institutions than the

[9] Wilber G. Katz, "Religion and American Constitutions," Julius Rosenthal Foundation Lecture, Northwestern University School of Law, March 21, 1963.

broad outlines of the First Amendment.[10] One reason that few school-aid problems have come to the United States Supreme Court is that the practices challenged in the courts have rarely survived the test of the various state constitutions, usually without additional reliance on the provisions of the First Amendment.[11]

The present prospect of increased federal school aid is giving a sizable practical dimension to First Amendment school-aid questions that heretofore have been largely symbolic. Accordingly, present discussion of the constitutionality and desirability of aid to parochial schools seems, by tacit understanding, to be in terms of federal aid and the federal constitution.

In discussions of the subject of federal aid to parochial schools the framing of the issue can be decisive. Thus, if one begins with the premise that the quality of education is low or that the present status of the principles that govern the relations between church and state is bad and that the federal government should do something about it, then one may more readily conclude that changes in favor of aid are acceptable or at least ought to be tried. On the other hand, if one begins with the premise that all is relatively well with church-state-school relations and phrases the issue in terms of a heavy burden of proof that must be sustained by those who would change the satisfactory terms of the present order (a burden that, almost by definition, cannot be discharged), then the issue irresistibly forecasts the conclusion.

Of course there are ways of framing the issue that do not inevitably determine the conclusion, and perhaps do not even assist in reaching it. Arguments in terms of "fairness" or "justice" seem to be of this order. Thus, the fact that parents who send their children

[10] The various state statutes are cited and classified in Note, 50 YALE L. J. 917 (1941); Note, 49 COLUM. L. REV. 968, 990 (1949).

[11] For example, Drinan, *The Constitutionality of Public Aid to Parochial Schools*, p. 59, nn. 5–6 *infra*, cites seven principal state cases that have considered the constitutionality of bus-transportation, free-textbook, and tuition-payment measures since the Supreme Court's *Everson* decision in 1947. Only one of these statutes survived its test under the state constitution. Snyder v. Town of Newton, 147 Conn. 374, 161 A.2d 770 (1960), *appeal dismissed for want of a substantial federal question*, 365 U.S. 299 (1961) (Frankfurter and Douglas, JJ., dissenting).

to private or parochial schools must pay taxes to support public schools that their religion or circumstances do not permit them to patronize is argued to be unjust. But this label is also affixed to the converse—that of compelling taxpayers to support schools that teach religious doctrines to which they do not subscribe. On this subject a dialogue on comparative degrees of injustice is not likely to be fruitful.

On the specific issue whether the First Amendment permits the federal government to make financial contributions to parochial education, many thoughtful observers accept, at least as regards indirect contributions, Professor Kurland's conclusion that "anyone suggesting that the answer, as a matter of constitutional law, is clear one way or the other is either deluding or deluded."[12]

Everyone who has made an objective examination of the practices and precedents before attempting to state an argument for or against the constitutionality of indirect aid to parochial schools has experienced the inconvenience of apparently contradictory authority. For example, those who deem such aid legal on the theory that it would simply aid students, schools, or education (instead of the sponsoring churches) have the task of explaining the essential difference between the proposed shouldering of some financial burdens of parochial schools and the concededly illegal payment of comparable sums directly to the sources of their present support. Others, who visualize a constitutional barrier to all financial aid to religion, are confronted by a multitude of examples of financial assistance from government to the educational establishments and students of organized religion. These advocates must therefore suggest acceptable distinctions between the allegedly objectionable forms of proposed aid and the constitutionally permissible forms, such as the furnishing of transportation services and released-time students to parochial schools.

Distinctions are made, but they are neither easy nor satisfying. Indeed, a recital of the whole list of executive, legislative, and judicial decisions on proposed aids to church-related schools, the approved and the unapproved, reads like a complicated settlement

[12] KURLAND, RELIGION AND THE LAW 111 (1962).

hammered out at the bargaining table after the give-and-take of negotiation, rather than the product of rational and consistent adjudications or opinions on the issue of constitutionality. Viewed as a whole, the terms of our present order seem to be governed, not by sharply focused judgments on what is constitutional, but rather by carefully balanced appraisals of what is desirable, or feasible, or politic—as if we were not yet ready as a people to come face to face with the answers to constitutional questions across the board. Perhaps we are not.

These are the ingredients of controversy. The issues are here discussed in general by Harold E. Fey and William Gorman, who give their respective views on "Problems of Church and State in the United States." The specific question, "The Constitutionality of Public Aid to Parochial Schools," is the subject of the conflicting opinions of Robert F. Drinan and Murray A. Gordon.

TAXATION

The relationship between taxation and religion is an old problem. At the time of Christ, for example, a supposed conflict between the requirements of religious law and the demands of the tax collector was thought to pose an insoluble dilemma—a convenient device for leading an unpopular person into making a statement that could be used to condemn him under the religious law or deliver him over to the civil authority for advocating disobedience to Rome. So it was that the chief priests and scribes came to Jesus and submitted this question:

Is it lawful to give tribute unto Caesar, or not?
But Jesus perceived their wickedness, and said, Why tempt ye me, ye hypocrites?
Shew me the tribute money. And they brought unto him a penny.
And he saith unto them, Whose is this image and superscription?
They say unto him, Caesar's. Then saith he unto them, Render therefore unto Caesar the things which are Caesar's; and unto God the things that are God's.[13]

[13] *Matt.* 22:17–22; *Mark* 12:13–17; *Luke* 20:19–26.

Today, over nineteen hundred years later, this familiar aphorism is still quoted—and some of the chief priests and scribes are still worried about the superscriptions on coins.

One of the strangest anomalies in the modern framework of church-state relations is the apparent willingness of those who protest even the smallest state recognition or aid of religion to accept without litigation the massive governmental subsidy inherent in the various tax concessions to religious organizations.

An examination of the origin of exemptions from state and local property taxes reveals them to be a vestige of the early established churches. Almost all of the original thirteen states had established churches or religions.[14] So long as a church was supported by taxes its property was exempt from taxation for the same reason as other public property. When the Establishments were discontinued early in the nineteenth century, the exemption of church property was so completely in accord with popular sentiment that it continued unchanged and was later formalized in statutory and constitutional provisions.[15] Since the middle of the nineteenth century the wisdom of such exemptions has been repeatedly questioned,[16] but they have seldom been challenged in the courts.

Although the federal income-tax provisions favoring religious organizations are of more recent origin, they seem to have come into the law without any apparent concern for their effects as subsidies of organized religion. The provision exempting the income of religious corporations from taxation, which originated in the Revenue Act of 1916,[17] was enacted on Treasury recommendation because the securing of returns from such organizations had proved annoying and expensive and had resulted in the collection of little or no tax.[18]

[14] See COBB, THE RISE OF RELIGIOUS LIBERTY IN AMERICA chs. 3–6 (1902) ; Engel v. Vitale, 370 U.S. 421, 427–28 (1962).

[15] ZOLLMAN, AMERICAN CHURCH LAW §§ 344–46 (1933) ; Note, 49 COLUM. L. REV. 968 (1949).

[16] See Paulsen, *Preferment of Religious Institutions in Tax and Labor Legislation*, 14 LAW & CONTEMP. PROB. 144, 148–49 (1949).

[17] Revenue Act of 1916, ch. 463, § 11, 39 Stat. 756, 766.

[18] H.R. REP. No. 922, 64th Cong., 1st Sess. 4 (1916).

The provision awarding a deduction for contributions to religious organizations, introduced in the Revenue Act of 1917,[19] was one of a number of amendments suggested by the Treasury on the basis of its experience with the income tax, but it was not among the "more important amendments so recommended" that were explicitly discussed in the Committee Reports.[20] Neither the Committee Reports nor the Hearings on these Acts[21] contain any mention of a possible constitutional, political, or policy objection to the aid to religion inherent in the exemption and deduction provisions, and there appears to be no public record of any subsequent attempt to repeal them, even though each increase in the tax rate has made their impact more significant.

The apparent absence of challenge to the income-tax provisions in the courts cannot be dismissed as a mere corollary of the rule that neither individual taxpayers nor states have standing to make a justiciable challenge to federal appropriations.[22] In the first place, this rule was not established until six or seven years after the enactment of these provisions, and there is no record of any attempt to raise the constitutional question in the interim. In contrast, even after that rule was adopted, one litigant sought, albeit unsuccessfully, to enjoin the disbursement of funds for salaries of chaplains of the armed forces, Senate, and House of Representatives on the ground that this constituted a promotion of religious views and a forbidden establishment of religion.[23] In addition, the rule that precludes the individual taxpayer from enjoining an unconstitutional appropriation of funds does not preclude him from resisting the imposition of a tax that is part of an unconstitutional plan.[24]

[19] Revenue Act of 1917, ch. 63, § 1201, 40 Stat. 300, 330.

[20] S. Rep. No. 103, 65th Cong., 1st Sess. 20 (1917).

[21] Committee reports cited notes 18 and 20 *supra;* H.R. Rep. No. 45, 65th Cong., 1st Sess. (1917) ; S. Rep. No. 793, 64th Cong., 1st Sess. (1916) ; *Hearings on H.R. 4280 Before the Senate Committee on Finance,* 65th Cong., 1st Sess. (1917) ; *Hearings on H.R. 16763 Before a Subcommittee of the Senate Committee on Finance,* 64th Cong., 1st Sess. (1916).

[22] Massachusetts v. Mellon, 262 U.S. 447 (1923).

[23] Elliott v. White, 23 F.2d 997 (D.C. Cir. 1928).

[24] United States v. Butler, 297 U.S. 1, 57–58 (1936).

However unlikely the prospect of a successful challenge to the religious subsidy aspect of the federal income-tax laws, it is remarkable that there is no public record of such attempts.

In "The Constitutionality of Tax Exemptions for Religious Activities," Paul G. Kauper discusses the types of federal and state tax concessions, the arguments for and against such provisions, and the present and probable future status of constitutional law on this subject.

ADOPTION AND PLACEMENT

The polestar in questions of adoption and placement is the "welfare" or "best interests" of the child. In popular opinion, the type of religious instruction a foster child will receive is undoubtedly a major ingredient in such a formula. However, this religious factor is not one that courts can readily apply without consciously or unconsciously entering the forbidden domain of passing judgment on the merits of various religious faiths.

Possible constitutional objections and admitted practical difficulties in applying a religious factor in adoption proceedings have convinced some authorities that the subject of religion should be entirely omitted from adoption legislation. Thus, a considerable number of states have no religious factor in their adoption legislation, and a model state adoption act recently recommended by a federal agency omits any mention of religion.[25] This omission of religion as an independent factor does not reduce its practical importance in the adoption process or preclude its consideration by the court where appropriate to other objectives. For example, the religious factor has great extra-legal significance in the placement decisions of adoption agencies, particularly the denominational agencies that have such a prominent role in adoptions. In addition, the religious factor would sometimes be directly relevant to the court, as where the interests of avoiding emotional distress to a child who had received some religious training after attaining the age of

25 U.S. CHILDREN'S BUREAU, DEP'T OF HEALTH, EDUCATION AND WELFARE, LEGISLATIVE GUIDES FOR THE TERMINATION OF PARENTAL RIGHTS AND RESPONSIBILITIES AND THE ADOPTION OF CHILDREN 49 (1961), discussed in Katz, *Judicial and Statutory Trends in the Law of Adoption*, 62 GEO. L.J. 64 (1962).

discretion would dictate that he not be uprooted from that faith and trained in another.

Judging from the action of state legislatures, the predominant sentiment favors mandatory consideration of the religion of the parties in child adoptions. A great majority of our states have enacted what are commonly called "religious protection" statutes.[26] In form these provisions seem to avoid requiring a court to decide which type of religious instruction would serve the best interests of the child by imputing some denominational choice to the child and then by requiring the court to take steps to preserve the presumed status quo. Typically these statutes require that the court, "when practicable" or "whenever possible," give custody to a person or persons of the same religious "faith or persuasion" or "belief" as the child.

However, to impute a religious choice to an infant avoids the embarrassment of selecting one for him only if the basis for imputation is clear. It is clear in those cases where the child is old enough to have a "belief" or "persuasion." Moreover, since children usually follow the faith of their parents, a court can rationally impute to a child the denomination of both of his natural parents. In other circumstances the choice is not clear, and the uncertainties in the application of these statutes have vexed courts and litigants alike. For example, the natural parents will sometimes be of different faiths, or it may be impossible to determine their religious affiliation. In such cases should the court impute a denominational choice to an infant on the basis of membership acquired (according to church law) by birth or by some initiatory ordinance? Could this be done without conferring an impermissible legal advantage on those denominations that recognize membership by birth or those that have significant initiatory acts for infants? Another question that will sometimes arise in this situation is whether the court should give effect to an agreement between the parents as to the child's religious instruction.

The religious-protection statutes pose additional problems after

[26] The various state statutes are cited and discussed in Note, 54 COLUM. L. REV. 376, 396–403 (1954).

the child's denomination has been determined. There remains the necessity of determining the denominational choice of the adoptive parents, the effect of differences between the two of them, and the potentially embarrassing theological question whether their denomination is really "different" from that of the adopted child. Of course the "whenever possible" reservation in the statutes preserves flexibility by giving the judge some discretion (at least theoretically) to award custody to adoptive parents of a faith different from the child, but the statutes have generally left to the courts the task of defining when this would be appropriate. In addition, the statutes also invite litigation by being unclear on whether the court discharges its obligation by awarding custody to parents of the desired religious faith or whether the court must also decree that the child shall be raised in the imputed faith even though the adoptive parents change their allegiance.

The inherent problems and the apparent effect of the religious-protection statutes may lead some to conclude that the statutes were well named: they are designed more for the protection of religion than for the benefit of the child.

The "Constitutional Problems of Utilizing a Religious Factor in Adoptions and Placements of Children" are treated by Monrad G. Paulsen.

PRAYER

It has been suggested that the church-state problem is only one aspect of the larger question of what role religion should play in public life, and, in turn, that this question cannot be answered without some definition of the role of religion in the life of the individual.[27] If this is so, then we may expect little relief from church-state problems until a large proportion of those who make up the churches and the state are able to define the place of religion in their own lives. It also seems to follow from the suggested hypothesis that the current points of public friction in this area have

27 RELIGION AND AMERICAN SOCIETY 10–11 (Center for the Study of Democratic Institutions 1961).

their basic causes, or at least their counterparts, in certain religious conflicts or uncertainties in the minds of men.

The apparent concern with certain public religious symbols seems to be an example of this. A familiar occurrence around Christmas is the furor touched off by attempts to establish or prohibit a crèche on public property. A more common, if less vocal, controversy relates to the use of the name of Deity on coins or on public places or documents. Some deem this a dangerous portent of intolerance for the unbeliever. Others see great positive merit in such manifestations, as if these symbols, like some expiatory act, somehow make us, as a nation or as a people, better or more religious than we really are. There seems to be some hope, or fear, that the inclusion of the name of God on coins or in the Declaration of Independence or Pledge of Allegiance somehow proves that we are a religious people, or that the omission of His name from the Constitution somehow establishes that we are not. Other religionists, even those who would not approve changing traditional inclusions (or omissions), may resent reliance on such symbolism, believing that if we are, or are to become, a religious people it will be by acts of devotion and faith, not by Acts of Congress.

One of the curious things about these public symbols is that they have not evoked more protest from religious people who sense that official governmental participation in essentially religious activities carries grave danger of leading to some sort of orthodox national religion that would dilute or debase the tenets of existing faiths, particularly those who believe in one "true" church. For many persons and denominations, various religions are not like so many fractions that appear different but are all susceptible of being reduced to some lowest common denominator without impairing their meaning or value.

The most celebrated public symbol of recent times was the New York Regents' prayer.[28] From the great hue and cry that arose against the Supreme Court's decision in this case[29] it would seem

[28] "Almighty God, we acknowledge our dependence upon Thee, and we beg Thy blessings upon us, our parents, our teachers and our Country."

[29] Engel v. Vitale 370 U.S. 421 (1962).

that many religious people favor beginning the school day with a standard, compulsory, public prayer. Other religious parents may prefer that their children be educated according to a different standard:

> And when thou prayest, thou shalt not be as the hypocrites are: for they love to pray standing in the synagogues and in the corners of the streets, that they may be seen of men. Verily I say unto you, They have their reward.
>
> But thou, when thou prayest, enter into thy closet, and when thou hast shut thy door, pray to thy Father which is in secret; and thy Father which seeth in secret shall reward thee openly.[30]

In other words, for some readers of this passage there may be spiritual, as well as constitutional and educational, objections to the Regents' prayer.

It seems odd that the Regents' form of words, which was imposed upon children in the guise of worship, drew so much fire from parents for its allegedly subversive theology, and so little for its religious sterility. It is also surprising that the churchmen who attacked the Supreme Court so vociferously for its decision that "it is no part of the business of government to compose official prayers for any group of the American people to recite as a part of a religious program carried on by government"[31] were not more sensitive to the fact that the same powers that could prescribe prayer might eventually induce or compel orthodoxy. The voices of moderation were soon heard from the religious community, however, and resignation to the result was soon followed by substantial support for the Court's position. A number of prominent religious organizations and individuals, anticipating further restrictions in the Lord's-Prayer and Bible-reading cases, even issued statements apparently or avowedly designed to reduce public opposition to the rulings.[32] When the Supreme Court finally issued its opinions in these cases, just as this volume was going to press, the public re-

[30] *Matt.* 6:5–6.

[31] 370 U.S. at 425.

[32] *E.g.*, see Lewis, *High Court Ruling on School Prayer May Come Today*, N.Y. Times, June 17, 1963, p. 1, col. 3 (city ed.) ; *3 Clerics Ask Public: Accept Bible Rulings*, Chicago Tribune, June 4, 1963, p. 9, col. 4, sec. 2.

sponse—by comparison with the reaction to the Regents'-prayer case a year earlier—was almost temperate.

My colleague Philip B. Kurland, whose book, *Religion and the Law,* has attracted such wide attention, discusses the factual and legal background and effect of the prayer cases in the concluding chapter, "The School Prayer Cases."[33] The effective service of Professor Kurland and his committee in the arrangement and conduct of the Law School's Conference on Church and State, and his own valuable counsel in the preparation of this book, are gratefully acknowledged.

Dallin H. Oaks*

[33] Of the various contributors to this volume, only Professor Kurland had the benefit of study of the Supreme Court's decisions in the Lord's-Prayer and Bible-reading cases. Owing to the exigencies of press deadlines, the earlier chapters were submitted some months before the Court's decisions of June 17, 1963.

* Dallin H. Oaks is Associate Professor of Law, The University of Chicago.

ROBERT M. HUTCHINS

The Future of the Wall

Its past has not been brilliant; its future is not bright. It first appeared in the opinion of Mr. Chief Justice Waite, in *Reynolds v. United States*,[1] where it played no role in the decision that interference with religious polygamy was not interference with religious freedom. The wall arose in this context because the Chief Justice wanted to use another phrase in Jefferson's letter to support his decision: he could not edit the letter to leave out the wall. The remark of Jefferson on which the Chief Justice relied was that the powers of government could reach only the actions of men, not their opinions.[2] Since polygamy was an action, and an unpopular one at that, it was open to the government to deny the defendant enjoyment of it, even though he alleged that he was authorized, or even ordered, by his church to commit it.

All was quiet along the wall until *Everson v. Board of Education*.[3] It assumed massive proportions then and has been growing ever since. Its growth has, however, been largely literary and ornamental.

ROBERT M. HUTCHINS is President of the Fund for the Republic, Inc., and Chairman of the Consultants to the Center for the Study of Democratic Institutions. This paper is also published in substance in 108 AMERICA 146 (1963).

[1] 98 U.S. 145, 164 (1878).

[2] Jefferson's January 1, 1802 letter to the Danbury Baptist Association is quoted in 8 THE WRITINGS OF THOMAS JEFFERSON 113 (Washington ed. 1861).

[3] 330 U.S. 1, 16, 18 (1947).

It has not produced those instant solutions which its apparent clarity and directness lead its devotees to expect. In the *Everson* case, for example, the wall did not prevent the state from giving assistance, at least in the form of bus rides, to children attending parochial schools, even though four justices could see it blocked these payments; and in *Zorach v. Clauson*[4] a far from unanimous court let the New York program of released time through the wall. But almost every justice feels constrained to bow before it.

Only Mr. Justice Reed, dissenting in *McCollum v. Board of Education*,[5] has argued much against it. In that case Mr. Justice Frankfurter, concurring, raised the wall to new heights of eloquence by saying, "Separation means separation, not something less. Jefferson's metaphor in describing the relation between Church and State speaks of a 'wall of separation,' not of a fine line easily overstepped."[6]

Mr. Justice Reed replied, "A rule of law should not be drawn from a figure of speech."[7] He pointed out that Jefferson's letter says religion is a matter between a man and his God; he owes account of it to none other; and the powers of government reach actions only. He could not see in these propositions any clear prohibition against the released-time program in Champaign. On the contrary, he suggested, Jefferson himself, with Madison's approval, had worked out a scheme by which the University of Virginia could see to it that all students received religious instruction.

The wall-builders on the Court may be accused of misplaced piety. Their devotional sentiments might better have been directed to the Constitution—which speaks only of the prohibition of establishment and the exercise of freedom—than to words appearing in what may have been a routine acknowledgment of a complimentary address, words written by a man, however great, who did not take part in the adoption of the First Amendment. The same may be said of Mr. Justice Frankfurter's quotation in the *McCollum* case from General Grant,[8] who there receives what must be the first tribute ever paid him as a political philosopher.

[4] 343 U.S. 306 (1952).   [6] *Id.* at 231.
[5] 333 U.S. 203 (1948).   [7] *Id.* at 247.   [8] *Id.* at 218.

The wall has done what walls usually do: it has obscured the view. It has lent a simplistic air to the discussion of a very complicated matter. Hence it has caused confusion whenever it has been invoked. Far from helping to decide cases, it has made opinions and decisions unintelligible. The wall is offered as a reason. It is not a reason; it is a figure of speech.

The problems of Mr. Justice Jackson are instructive. In *Everson v. Board of Education* he said in dissent: (1) Catholic education is the rock (another unfortunate metaphor) upon which the Catholic Church rests, and aid to a Catholic school is the same as aid to the Church. (2) "Our public school, if not a product of Protestantism, at least is more consistent with it than with the Catholic culture and scheme of values."[9] This would mean that supporting public schools is supporting Protestant churches, or at least something that by being "more consistent" with them tends to lend them support. (3) Public education is organized on the premise that education "can be isolated from all religious teaching so that the school can inculcate all needed temporal knowledge and also maintain a strict and lofty neutrality as to religion."[10] Mr. Justice Jackson adds, it seems to me indefensibly: "Whether such a disjunction is possible, and if possible whether it is wise, are questions I need not try to answer."[11] A man who rests his opinion on the necessity of separation is bound to try to answer the question whether separation can, in fact, occur. If it cannot occur, then, according to his own doctrine, the state will be supporting religious teaching.

Concurring in the *McCollum* case, Mr. Justice Jackson went in even deeper. There he said:

I think it remains to be demonstrated whether it is possible, even if desirable, . . . completely to isolate and cast out of secular education all that some people may reasonably regard as religious instruction. . . . The fact is, that for good or for ill, nearly everything in our culture worth transmitting, everything which gives meaning to life, is saturated with religious influences. . . .

But how one can teach, with satisfaction or even with justice to all faiths, such subjects as the story of the Reformation, the Inquisition, or even the New England effort to found "a Church without a Bishop and

[9] 330 U.S. at 23.   [10] *Id.* at 24.   [11] *Ibid.*

a State without a King," is more than I know. . . . When instruction turns to proselyting and imparting knowledge becomes evangelism is, except in the crudest cases, a subtle inquiry. . . .

It is idle to pretend that this task is one for which we can find in the Constitution one word to help us as judges to decide where the secular ends and the sectarian begins in education. Nor can we find guidance in any other legal source. It is a matter on which we can find no law but our own prepossessions. If with no surer legal guidance we are to take up and decide every variation of this controversy . . . we are likely to have much business of the sort. And, more importantly, we are likely to make the legal "wall of separation between church and state" as winding as the famous serpentine wall designed by Mr. Jefferson for the University he founded.[12]

And sure enough, in the *Zorach* case, Mr. Justice Jackson found that "[t]he wall which the Court was professing to erect between Church and State has become even more warped and twisted than I expected."[13] A man who proposes to erect a wall in the midst of a saturated solution and have the material on one side different from that on the other should not be surprised at the failure of his experiment.

Like Mr. Justice Jackson, the Educational Policies Commission holds that "knowledge about religion is essential for a full understanding of our culture, literature, art, history and current affairs."[14] But if knowledge about religion is to be communicated, it will presumably be communicated by somebody who has a view of the subject and who cannot be expected to conceal it. If he is paid by the state, what has happened to the wall?

As Mr. Justice Jackson suggests, the wall is really a permeable membrane and is getting more porous all the time. The well-worn catalogue of so-called aids to religion that Mr. Justice Reed began in the *McCollum* case and that Justices Douglas and Stewart reiterated in *Engel v. Vitale*[15] is getting longer every day. Whenever public policy seems to require the expenditure of public funds for

[12] 333 U.S. at 335–38.   [13] 343 U.S. at 325.

[14] Quoted in Religion in American Society 47 (Center for the Study of Democratic Institutions 1961).

[15] 370 U.S. 421 (1962).

a public purpose, the incidental "aid to religion," if any, is disregarded. This has been held true of bus transportation, free textbooks, and hospitals. It is true of aid under the G.I. Bill of Rights, of school lunches, of expenditures under the National Defense Education Act, of scholarships and fellowships awarded by public agencies—some of which are granted to theological schools. And certiorari was denied when New York helped Fordham University acquire land in Lincoln Center at less than cost.[16] As non-discriminatory tax exemption, which is solid financial aid, has never been successfully challenged when granted a church or church schools, so financial aid directed to a public purpose other than the support of religion has never been struck down by the United States Supreme Court, even when the financial benefit to religious organizations was obvious.

This is as it should be. When something has to be done through schools, colleges, and universities, it would be self-defeating to try to act as though schools, colleges, and universities under religious auspices did not exist and did not have innumerable students, teachers, and scholars who ought to be involved. If it is objected that non-believers are thereby taxed to aid religion, the answer is that by hypothesis the aid to religion is incidental to an overriding public benefit that cannot be obtained without including institutions under religious auspices and that, since the object of the religion clauses of the First Amendment is to guarantee and promote religious freedom, such incidental benefits, which do not limit religious freedom, do not invalidate the legislation.

Federal aid to education is inevitable, and the sooner it comes the better. The flagrant injustice, to say nothing of shortsightedness, in committing the support of education to fifty states characterized by wide economic disparities and highly mobile populations requires no elaboration here. Federal aid has arrived in a large way by the back door. Its formal admission through the main entrance cannot be long delayed.

Federal aid should go to all educational institutions that meet

[16] 64th St. Residences, Inc. v. City of New York, 4 N.Y.2d 268, 150 N.E.2d 396, 174 N.Y.S.2d 1 (1958), *cert. denied,* 357 U.S. 907 (1958).

federal standards. Mr. Justice Jackson is wrong in saying a school is a church if it is managed by a church and is important to its religious work. A school is an educational institution and not a church if its object is intellectual development and if it is engaged, bona fide, in this task. The fact that it is owned by a church or that it gives some religious instruction or that its teaching is "permeated" by religion or that aid to it is incidentally of some benefit to the church is immaterial. Aid to all educational institutions that meet federal standards would promote religious freedom as well as education. The overriding public purpose would be to improve education, including education in institutions under religious auspices. Supporting them would no more be a violation of the First Amendment than it would be to hold institutions under religious auspices to federal standards as a condition of receiving federal aid.

Since the object of the First Amendment is to guarantee and promote religious freedom, including freedom from religion, it is a violation of the Amendment to apply pressure, directly or indirectly, upon the conscience of any person. Such pressure may have been present, though Justices Douglas and Stewart did not detect it, in *Engel v. Vitale*. It may also lurk in the *Zorach* case and in *Doremus v. Board of Education*.[17] The "brief moment with eternity"[18] that the Supreme Court of New Jersey said the statute compelled every child to have every day is not within the competence of the state, and excusing any pupil in the Borough of Hawthorne upon request may substitute indirect for direct pressure. Distinctions among school children on the basis of their religion, or lack of it, are bound to seem invidious.

This brings us back to the perplexities of Mr. Justice Jackson. We may all agree that a school that children are compelled to attend should not hold religious ceremonies in which some children or their parents do not believe. But suppose the educational authorities, taking the hint from Mr. Justice Jackson and the Educational Policies Commission, decide that every child in such a school, before

[17] 342 U.S. 429 (1952).

[18] Doremus v. Board of Education, 5 N.J. 435, 451, 75 A.2d 880, 888 (1950), *appeal dismissed*, 342 U.S. 429 (1952).

he reaches the school-leaving age, must take a course in religion or in the history of religion or in comparative religion. Since the object is education and not the propagation of religion, no question can be raised about the support of religion or the invasion of religious freedom. The only questions are whether the course and the teacher are adequate. It is doubtful whether these are questions for the courts, or even for the legislature.

We need to learn what education is, and who is responsible for its general direction and its content. I suggest we might try to establish the distinction between edification, indoctrination, and education and then work toward the elimination of everything but education from educational institutions. My principal objection to the prayer considered in *Engel v. Vitale* is not constitutional; it is educational. The prayer was a part of the so-called moral training program of the Board of Regents. It had little or no value as such training. In any event, the primary responsibility of the Board of Regents is not moral training, which is the province of the family and the church, but education, which may supply the intellectual foundations of morality, but which does not attempt to convey its moral message by way of edification or indoctrination. In general we may say that a teacher who tries to indoctrinate his pupils is incompetent and should be subject to discipline from the proper quarter.

In *Pierce v. Society of Sisters*[19] the Court said the child was not the mere creature of the state. Is the school the mere creature of the state? We may admit the self-evident truth that an educational system supported by taxes cannot survive if it does not command the allegiance of the taxpayers. Does this mean that the policies and curriculum of schools are to be determined by the taxpayers?

Two ancient propositions are the starting point of any discussion of the autonomy of educational institutions. The first is: All men by nature desire to know. The second is: Politics is the architectonic science, which determines what shall be studied in the state. The first proposition is normative; the second is descriptive. Any actual educational system is judged by the degree to which it meets the

19 268 U.S. 510 (1925).

standard of the first proposition and makes it possible for all men to know. The free-speech, free-press, and free-assembly provisions of the First Amendment proclaim this ideal for the United States.

The New York Supreme Court, dismissing a suit to compel the Board of Education to remove *Oliver Twist* and *The Merchant of Venice* from school libraries and classrooms, said, "Educational institutions are concerned with the development of free inquiry and learning. The administrative officers must be free to guide teachers and pupils toward that goal. Their discretion must not be interfered with in the absence of proof of actual malevolent intent."[20]

Concurring in *Wieman v. Updegraff*,[21] Mr. Justice Frankfurter, joined by Mr. Justice Douglas, found that state and national power could not limit the functions of educational institutions, from the primary grades through the universities, by limiting the participation of teachers in "that restless, enduring process of extending the bounds of understanding and wisdom, to assure which the freedoms of thought, of speech, of inquiry, of worship are guaranteed by the Constitution of the United States against infraction by National or State government."[22]

The wall has no future. What has a future is the rational, non-metaphorical discussion, in the light of all the provisions of the First Amendment, of the methods by which we may guarantee and promote religious freedom and the methods by which we may obtain an educational system worthy of the potentialities and responsibilities of our people.

The First Amendment is a charter of learning. It confirms empowerments as well as immunities. We are to learn how to use our freedom. If we are to be metaphorical, let us recognize that the First Amendment is not intended as a fence, or wall, around a vacant lot. Something is supposed to be going on inside. What is supposed to be going on is learning. A political community is an educational life in process.

[20] Rosenberg v. Board of Education, 196 Misc. 542, 543–44, 92 N.Y.S.2d 344, 346 (Sup. Ct. 1949).

[21] 344 U.S. 183 (1952).   [22] *Id.* at 196–97.

The wall has no future because it cannot help us learn. If taken literally, it is arbitrary and unreasonable, pretending to separate things that are not in all respects separable, thwarting efforts to understand what education and freedom of (and from) religion demand, hampering us in our search for what we need above everything else—a national idea of education and a national program to carry it out.

If the West has a future, it is as the schoolmaster of the world. If democracy has a future, it lies in struggling to be what no big, advanced, industrial country has succeeded in becoming: a community learning together to govern itself and to achieve the common good. American participation in these great enterprises should not be obstructed by a figure of speech.

Problems of Church and State

in the United States:

A Protestant View

AN ARGUMENT FOR SEPARATION

Our traditional coexistence of church and state, each structurally independent of the other, is being tested, particularly in the fields of education and welfare. In a dynamic society the functions, and consequently the institutions, of state and church have expanded and begun to overlap. So the time has come for new definitions and measures of self-limitation. This paper is motivated by the belief that the religious covenant under which the church exists and the political covenant under which the state is maintained can and should be distinguished in the mind of the citizen and that the institutions that derive from these covenants should be kept legally separate.

Although the application of existing laws is not always clear and court tests are sometimes essential, I do not agree with Bishop James Pike of San Francisco that the First Amendment should be amended,[1] as he declared after the Supreme Court handed down its

THE REVEREND HAROLD E. FEY is Editor of THE CHRISTIAN CENTURY.

[1] See Smylie, *The First Amendment and Bishop Pike*, 79 CHRISTIAN CENTURY 1316 (1962).

decision in the Regents'-prayer case.[2] The First Amendment specifically limits the state and thus defines an area of freedom for the individual and the church. By setting bounds on the operation of the political covenant, it marks out the province of the religious covenant. This delimitation is an essential characteristic of a pluralistic society.

Evidence, in addition to the First Amendment, that the framers of the Constitution had in mind such a pluralistic order is found in the Ohio Constitution, adopted only a few years after the United States Constitution was written. Among the "general, great and essential principles of liberty and free government" which Article VIII of that 1802 document declares, in order that they "may be recognized and forever unalterably established," was the following:

That all men have a natural and indefeasible right to worship Almighty God according to the dictates of conscience; that no human authority can in any case whatever, control or interfere with the rights of conscience; that no man shall be compelled to attend, erect or support any place of worship, or to maintain any ministry against his consent, and that no preference shall ever be given, by law, to any religious society or mode of worship, and no religious test shall be required as a qualification to any office of trust or profit. But religion, morality and knowledge being essentially necessary to the good government and the happiness of mankind, schools and the means of instruction shall forever be encouraged by legislative provision, not inconsistent with the rights of conscience.[3]

That was the platform; what have been the results? The evolution of religious liberty, its institutionalization in the Constitution, and the successful development on a voluntary basis of various churches during our national history favorably impressed Alexis de Tocqueville, Ambassador James Bryce, Gunnar Myrdal, and a host of less eminent observers of the American Commonwealth. Today religion prospers. Nearly two-thirds of the American people are members of some church—a figure which Russell Kirk, writing in *Fortune* two years ago,[4] considered to be about as high as mem-

2 Engel v. Vitale, 370 U.S. 421 (1962).

3 OHIO CONST. art. VIII, § 3 (1802).

4 Kirk, *Can Protestantism Hold Its Own in a Modern America?* Fortune, Feb. 1961, p. 108.

bership on a voluntary basis is likely to go. While thoughtful people are concerned with raising the quality of religious devotion, its quantity also commands respect. In each of the last several years, members of churches have contributed around one billion dollars for new church buildings. Meanwhile they maintained hundreds of institutions of higher education, thousands of hospitals, parochial schools, homes for the aged and the orphaned, settlement houses, and other philanthropic enterprises. Before the Peace Corps was thought of, American Christians were supporting by voluntary contributions over twenty-five thousand workers in missions abroad, and American Jews were financing large development projects in Israel.

Meanwhile, this vital religious life was maintained voluntarily and on a basis of peace and order. So while there is admittedly room for improvement in the content and the expression of religion in this country, as well as in its contribution to civil society, the burden of proof rests on those who would change the terms on which church and state coexist in this land. Complacency is worse than a sin; it is a mistake, but we have ground for satisfaction in the results to date of the action of our fathers in including the principle of separation in the Constitution.

Where, then, are the church-state problems which concern us? Nobody is trying to establish a national church. No one seriously proposes to pay priests, rabbis, or ministers out of tax funds. We have not yet adopted a national creed, adherence to which is required on pain of imprisonment. Nobody is being taxed to support services of worship or to train ministers . . . or are they?

Dean M. Kelley of the Department of Religious Liberty of the National Council of Churches points out that most of the church-state issues emerge around the fringes of the question.[5] For example, he observes that ministries of religion are maintained by the state for military personnel. National Defense Education Act funds were granted to some theological seminaries for a while; the practice has now stopped. For many years pupils in the New York

[5] Address by Dean M. Kelley, "Religion and Public Education," Annual Conference of the Division of Christian Education of the National Council of Churches, Feb. 13, 1963.

schools were required by the Board of Regents of that state to pray
an officially composed prayer. Both houses of Congress and many
state institutions have chaplains. One of the academies training
officers of the armed services compels its men to attend chapel.
Some people are disturbed because church hospitals accept government funds under the Hill-Burton Act. Others see state involvement
in the tax exemption granted to churches.

We move closer to the center of the problem when we consider
church-state issues now before the courts. The variety of issues is
startling, coming after a long history of relative quiet. Writing in
a pamphlet published by the National Conference of Christians
and Jews, George R. La Noue, a doctoral candidate in political
science at Yale, points out that

> One hundred and fifty-eight years of constitutional history passed be-
> fore the United States Supreme Court first confronted the establish-
> ment clause of the First Amendment (Everson v. Board of Education,
> 330 U.S. 1). . . .
> Last year, however, from the spring of 1961 to the summer closing
> of the Court this year [1962], no less than seven cases involving the
> establishment clause were decided, and at least three more await the
> Court's return in the fall. In addition, church and state cases in the
> states numbered twoscore or more.[6]

Developments of the last year, outlined by Mr. La Noue, include
a case in which the Vermont high court decided against use of state
funds to pay the tuition of a pupil in a parochial school.[7] A Georgia
trial court held that a private school was non-sectarian in the meaning of the law, so could receive state funds, but the judgment was
reversed by the Georgia Supreme Court because the plaintiff had
not first exhausted available administrative remedies.[8] A Kentucky
court held that in a welfare case a state tuition grant could be given

[6] LA NOUE, A REVIEW OF CHURCH-STATE LEGAL DEVELOPMENTS 1961–62,
1 (Background Reports, National Conference of Christians and Jews, Sept.
1962).

[7] Swart v. South Burlington Town School Dist., 122 Vt. 177, 167 A.2d 514
(1961), cert. denied, 366 U.S. 925 (1961).

[8] Aikens v. O'Callahan, No. A89595, Super. Ct. Fulton County, Jan. 23,
1962, rev'd on other grounds, 218 Ga. 46, 126 S.E.2d 213 (1962).

to a cripple attending a non-sectarian private institution.[9] In Oregon the state supreme court outlawed a textbook law which had for twenty years been the basis on which the state had paid for text-books for parochial schools.[10] Alaskan and Wisconsin courts ruled against providing school-bus transportation for students of paro-chial schools.[11]

The most famous case of the year was *Engel v. Vitale*,[12] the New York Regents'-prayer case. The Supreme Court ruled that "it is no part of the business of government to compose official prayers for any group of the American people to recite as a part of a religious program carried on by government."[13] The decision produced an uproar which was remarkably violent and which subsided with a speed even more remarkable. In Maryland the Court of Appeals voted 4 to 3 to reject a protest against a 1905 Baltimore Board of School Commissioners rule requiring daily reading of a chapter of the Bible "and/or" use of the Lord's Prayer in school.[14] The case is now pending in the United States Supreme Court.[15] The section of the Pennsylvania Public School Code that requires read-ing of at least ten verses of the Bible at the opening of each school day was declared unconstitutional by a United States District Court.[16] This case is also pending in the Supreme Court.[17] A Florida court outlawed the distribution of Bibles through the public

[9] Butler v. United Cerebral Palsy of Northern Kentucky, Inc., 352 S.W.2d 203 (Ky. 1961).

[10] Dickman v. School Dist., 366 P.2d 533 (Ore. 1961), *cert. denied*, 371 U.S. 823 (1962).

[11] Matthews v. Quinton, 362 P.2d 932 (Alaska 1961), *appeal dismissed and cert. denied*, 368 U.S. 517 (1962); Reynolds v. Nusbaum, 17 Wis. 2d 148, 115 N.W.2d 761 (1962).

[12] 370 U.S. 421 (1962).   [13] *Id.* at 425.

[14] Murray v. Curlett, 228 Md. 239, 179 A.2d 698 (1962).

[15] *Ibid.*, *cert. granted*, 371 U.S. 809 (1962). (The Maryland court was re-versed. See Kurland, *The School Prayer Cases*, p. 158 *infra.*—ED.)

[16] Schempp. v. School District of Abington, 201 F. Supp. 815 (E. D. Pa. 1962).

[17] *Ibid.*, *prob. juris. noted*, 371 U.S. 807 (1962). (The lower court was affirmed. See Kurland, *supra* note 15, at 158.—ED.)

schools.[18] Another Florida judge upheld the constitutionality in
the public school of daily Bible reading, recitation of the Lord's
Prayer, singing of religious hymns and holding of baccalaureate
programs, but enjoined sectarian comments on the Bible by public
school teachers, use of school premises for after-school Bible instruction, exhibition of religious films, and religious observance
of Christmas, Easter, and Hanukkah holidays. The judgment was
affirmed by the Florida Supreme Court.[19] A Maryland law enacted
in its present form in 1867, which required belief in God as a
condition for holding public office, was overthrown.[20] Other cases
before various courts involved Sunday-closing and birth-control
laws.[21]

In Wisconsin the attorney general held that because the words
"under God" had been added to the Pledge of Allegiance, the state
law requiring recitation of the Pledge in school violated the First
and Fourteenth amendments.[22] In other official opinions by attor-
neys general, Kentucky deemed a released-time program offensive
to the Constitution, but North Dakota gave another such program
its blessing; Washington, in one of the first state rulings of its
kind, forbade public school districts from participating in the
planning, promotion, or execution of religious baccalaureate exercises; the wearing of sectarian garb in the public school classrooms
was upheld in Colorado, but the New York State Commissioner of
Education ruled that garbed nuns could not appear on the state's
educational television network.[23]

[18] Brown v. Orange County Bd. of Pub. Instruction, 128 So.2d 181 (Fla.
Dist. Ct. App. 1960), *cert. denied,* 129 So. 2d 141 (Fla. 1961).

[19] Chamberlin v. Dade County Bd. of Pub. Instruction, 143 So. 2d 21 (Fla.
1962), *appeal docketed,* 31 U.S.L. Week 3158 (U.S. Oct. 15, 1962) (No.
520). (The Florida judgment was vacated and remanded for reconsideration
in light of the Supreme Court's decisions in the cases cited notes 15 and 17
supra. 83 Sup. Ct. 1864 [1963].—ED.)

[20] Torcaso v. Watkins, 367 U.S. 488 (1961).

[21] McGowan v. Maryland, 366 U.S. 420 (1961); Poe v. Ullman, 367 U.S.
497 (1961).

[22] LA NOUE, *op. cit. supra* note 6, at 10.

[23] *Id.* at 12.

Another issue that may well find its way before the courts for adjudication is the practice, observed in over five hundred instances, of the giving or sale below market value of land and other property declared surplus by the government to religious denominations and their affiliates.[24] Property worth many millions of dollars has been given to Catholic and Protestant churches or church institutions, the gifts constituting what might well be considered support by government of establishments of religion. How do these gifts accord with the language used by the Supreme Court in its 1947 *Everson* opinion?

The "establishment of religion" clause of the First Amendment means at least this: Neither a state nor the Federal Government can set up a church. Neither can pass laws which aid one religion, aid all religions, or prefer one religion over another. Neither can force nor influence a person to go to or to remain away from church against his will or force him to profess a belief or disbelief in any religion. No person can be punished for entertaining or professing religious beliefs or disbeliefs, for church attendance or non-attendance. No tax in any amount, large or small, can be levied to support any religious activities or institutions, whatever they may be called, or whatever form they may adopt to teach or practice religion. Neither a state nor the Federal Government can, openly or secretly, participate in the affairs of any religious organizations or groups and *vice versa*. In the words of Jefferson, the clause against establishment of religion by law was intended to erect "a wall of separation between church and State."[25]

Those who at first contended that this statement was obiter dicta no longer make that contention, since the same language has appeared in Supreme Court decisions on five occasions over a fifteen-year period during which the personnel of the Court has almost totally changed, the latest use being in 1961 in the *Torcaso* case.[26] In view of the Court's frequent repetition of its statement banning governmental support of religious activities and institutions from tax funds, it seems highly unlikely that the Supreme Court would approve of grants to such activities and institutions of public prop-

[24] See Editorial, *Giveaway Program Continues*, 79 CHRISTIAN CENTURY 1553 (1962).

[25] Everson v. Board of Education, 330 U.S. 1, 15–16 (1947).

[26] Torcaso v. Watkins, 367 U.S. 488, 492–93 (1961).

erty originally purchased by the expenditure of tax funds. In antici-
pation of this, the executive branch of the federal government has
practically conceded the unconstitutionality of some of these give-
aways.[27]

What shall we make of the sudden great increase of agitation
and litigation over relations of church and state? Considering the
events of 1961–1962, which La Noue calls "the most important
single year in the legal history of American church and state relations,"[28] and considering the prospect that coming years will see
an increase in such activity, some people have concluded with
Bishop Pike that the fault lies in the inadequacy of our basic law.
Most Protestants do not accept this interpretation, and I do not.
We find the causes in the coincidence of several factors, which include an increased concern over the assertion and protection of
civil rights generally and the emergence of voluntary organizations
whose purpose is to champion these rights. La Noue estimates that
roughly half of the church-state cases are now presented or aided
in some way by such groups as the American Civil Liberties Union,
the American Jewish Congress, Protestants and Other Americans
United for Separation of Church and State, the National Catholic
Welfare Conference, and Citizens for Educational Freedom, the
latter a recently formed Catholic organization.[29] In addition, each
major decision of the Supreme Court produces additional litigation
in areas where past law has seemed to vary with each new ruling
of the Court.

The big cause, however, is not in the interpretation of law but
in the formulation of policy having to do with the proper role of

[27] The Department of Health, Education, and Welfare's *Memorandum on
the Impact of the First Amendment to the Constitution upon Federal Aid to
Education,* submitted to the Senate Subcommittee on Education, Committee
on Labor and Public Welfare, stated: "A more difficult case is the program
for the disposal of surplus Government property which includes sectarian
institutions. Certainly, measured by the criteria set out in this memorandum,
this program has in some instances approached and, it can be argued, has
even transgressed constitutional boundaries." Sen. Doc. No. 29, 87th Cong.,
1st Sess. 23 n.18 (1961), reprinted in 50 GEO. L.J. 349, 375–76 n.18 (1961).

[28] LA NOUE, *op. cit. supra* note 6, at 17.

[29] *Ibid.*

religion in education. The nineteenth-century compromise between religion and education secularized the public schools but concealed the fact by allowing some miscellaneous religious traditions and expressions to survive unchallenged. Now the challenge is being laid down to these compromises by liberal Protestants, by Jews, and by non-believers, some of whom seek to bar churches from exerting any influence in public education. On the other hand, the Catholic hierarchy and, more recently, some conservative Jews have engaged in a determined effort to gain support from public funds in one way or another for their parochial schools. As part of this campaign, Catholics have blocked bills for federal aid to public education for the last eighteen years in the hope that parochial schools would be included. The hope has proved to be a vain one. The issue is clear and the deadlock is complete. "Shared time" offers almost the only possibility of compromise.

In this situation we are going to have to fight out once more the issue of the nature of our society. Let us hope the conflict can be carried out peacefully in forums, in election contests, in contests before the courts. The Protestant view, if one can be said to exist and if I understand it, is shared by many Jews. It is that in this land the religious and the political covenants are and should be kept separated and that this separation should extend to the institutions of church and state and their means of support. Since we believe that the First Amendment and its corollary statements in the state constitutions are necessary for the maintenance of a pluralistic society, we intend to defend them.

The dominant view among Catholics and their allies, if I understand it, is that these laws are the product of earlier Protestant domination and may and should be changed. So the die is cast. Each side is organizing and should organize. Each has the duty to make its organizations responsible and to insist that they carry on the contest within the rules of democratic decision-making. This is exactly the sort of controversy with which the machinery of democracy is best equipped to deal. Its use will demonstrate that democracy will not break down unless it is short-circuited.

Under these circumstances, it is advisable that citizens of varying viewpoints confer and debate wherever possible to define issues and points of view. Determination to clarify questions on which Americans differ widely will create a demand for better reporting and more careful study of the issues. As we struggle to review and update our laws and relationships, we should become more conscious of the crucial role which the courts must play and of the necessity for us to support the judiciary in the discharge of its essential function. The overt violations of law by officials and the embittered and untruthful campaigns of propaganda against the courts that we have seen and heard in recent years should provide all the incentive the legal and clerical professions need to unite them in upholding respect for the law and the courts. At the same time, the controversy, the outcome of which will determine the nature of our society, should be the concern of all.

This is the issue we cannot evade. We must rediscover and renew our devotion to the ideal and practice of a pluralistic society which is implicit in the Constitution and particularly in the First Amendment. As a philosophic principle, pluralism is the opposite of monism, and it differs from dualism. In social practice, pluralism expects so-called ultimates to maintain their character and yet to dwell side by side in the same society; it leaves to the people the voluntary choice of which of these ultimates, if any, will triumph. To invoke a term which is familiar in another context, a pluralistic society is an order of "disciplined coexistence." It is an order of self-limitaton, of refusing to go over the brink to destroy or falsely to undermine your opponent. In a pluralist society varying religious systems, each claiming some unique form of access to ultimate truth, peacefully contend and coexist with one another and with those who maintain a secularistic or atheistic position. In addition, all citizens have an obligation to maintain the pluralistic order.

While it would obviously be impossible for the state to support a single religious establishment in a pluralistic society, some of our citizens still insist that the state could and should support a multiple establishment by aiding all religions equally. People who believe that the state should, for example, extend equal or proportionate aid to all parochial schools understand neither the political nor the religious covenants on which our society is built. Such state support is impossible because it undercuts both religious and political liberty. The practical difficulty of this position is illustrated if we ask what response could be made by the state to a request for support of the parochial schools of the Black Muslim society, which claims to be a religion, or of any other extremist cult. I will return to this point later.

Separation of church and state was originally held to be valid because of an essentially religious conception of the nature of man. For example, Roger Williams, whom Professor Brockunier described as the "earliest of the fathers of American democracy," wrote in 1644:

> [A]ll civil states with their officers of justice in their respective constitutions and administrations are proved essentially civil, and therefore not judges, governors, or defenders of the spiritual or Christian state or worship. . . .
> [A]n enforced uniformity of religion throughout a nation or civil state, confounds the civil and religious, denies the principles of Christianity and civility, and that Jesus Christ is come in the flesh.[30]

A half-century after Roger Williams (1685), John Locke wrote in the same vein:

> The toleration of those that differ from others in matters of religion is so agreeable to the Gospel of Jesus Christ, and to the genuine reason of mankind, that it seems monstrous for men to be so blind as not to perceive the necessity and advantage of it in so clear a light. . . .
> [T]he care of souls cannot belong to the civil magistrate, because his power consists only in outward force; but true and saving religion consists in the inward persuasion of the mind, without which nothing can be acceptable to God.[31]

Nearly a century further down this widening stream of freedom came the Virginia Bill of Rights, phrased by Madison in language which owed much to the Magna Charta, to the acts of the Long

[30] Williams, *A Plea for Religious Liberty*, 1 THE PEOPLE SHALL JUDGE 21 (1949).

[31] Locke, *Letter Concerning Toleration*, in *id.* at 118–19.

Parliament, and to the doctrines of the Revolution of 1688 as interpreted by Locke. It held

That religion or the duty which we owe to our Creator, and the manner of discharging it, can be directed only by reason and conviction, not by force or violence; and, therefore, all men are equally entitled to the free exercise of religion, according to the dictates of conscience; and that it is the mutual duty of all to practice Christian forbearance, love, and charity toward each other."[32]

Finally, Maritain, the Catholic philosopher, has declared that "the founders of the American democracy were guided both by a Christian philosophy of life and by the Lockian tradition. . . ."[33]

It was this concept of basic distinction and difference between religious and political covenants which caused ten states of this commonwealth voluntarily to abandon their establishments of religion before the middle of the 1830's. It was this conviction which caused the nullification and repeal of laws which placed Catholics under civil disabilities in many colonies and states. It was this principle which choked off the Know-Nothing Movement, even though it was unable to prevent mobs in Boston, New York, Baltimore, and Cincinnati from taking lives. It was this faith which rooted religious liberty in state constitutions and gradually freed public schools from ecclesiastical direction. It was this which kept the entire nineteenth century free, with one exception (Massachusetts, 1826), from passing laws requiring the reading of the Bible in public schools. The state Bible-reading laws which are now under challenge are nearly all products of the twentieth century.[34]

It is this conviction which we are now told is out of date and must be abandoned. We are told that the wall of separation about which Jefferson spoke in describing the First Amendment has no future. The term "wall" as Jefferson used it means a distinction, a limitation, a definition of fields of competence and authority. The separation is not between people, dividing them into religious or

[32] Quoted in BATES, RELIGIOUS LIBERTY: AN INQUIRY 213 (1945).

[33] MARITAIN, THE TWILIGHT OF CIVILIZATION 58 (1943).

[34] JOHNSON & YOST, SEPARATION OF CHURCH AND STATE IN THE UNITED STATES 33 (1948).

ideological ghettos between which there can be no communication. It is primarily an idea in the mind of the citizen as he distinguishes between his obligations in separated fields. It clarifies rather than confuses thought, and it encourages rather than discourages dialogue between citizens. It is a line between two orders of experience, between absolutes on one side and relativities on the other, between the deep issues of faith and the practical issues of politics. It separates two realms of authority, each of which functions best when the two are distinguished. Finally, it bounds two systems of economics: the compulsory economy of a commonwealth and the voluntary economy of philanthropy.

If we remember with appreciation the benefits which have blessed church and state by their separation, we have equally strong reason to view with apprehension any form of institutional identification, merger, or union. If we now try to merge the compulsory element of government with the voluntary element of religion, we will do more than break down an outmoded verbal distinction. We will compromise individual freedom and disrupt public order. We will destroy a historic basis of peaceable relations between various forms of religious faith. We will undermine our system of public education, and we will make the state the determiner of what is and what is not religious. This is the way it could easily happen:

First, if we vote to grant subventions from tax funds to parochial schools, some citizens will conclude with reason that their individual freedom is violated because they are compelled to pay taxes for the support of religious ideas which they believe to be false. At first a few and later a great many citizens will refuse to pay such taxes. Attempts to coerce them will only spread disaffection.

Second, subvention of parochial schools from public funds will give an advantage to the denomination which has the largest system of parochial schools. Seeing this, denominations which have few or no sectarian schools will feel that if they are to survive they must also build such schools and claim their share of public funds for this purpose. If there is any more effective way of undermining public education than financing a multiplicity of sectarian systems from the public treasury, it has not been brought forward. This would especially be the case because such concessions would not purchase peace. The experience of France since 1905 and of other countries shows that the ecclesiastical appetite for public funds grows more rapidly than any legislature can vote appropriations to satisfy.

Finally, and most importantly, any attempt to merge the compulsory economy of the state with the voluntary economy of the church would force the state to make decisions which it is incompetent to make. A decision that the state must support all religious establishments equitably would bring applications from such fringe organizations as the Black Muslim Society. This society maintains parochial schools, in which colored children are taught to hate white people and to demand as a right the cession of territory on which a segregated state could be organized. Confronted by such an application, the government would be compelled to decide whether or not the Black Muslim Society is a religious body. The issue would inevitably be decided by the courts. Out of a succession of such decisions made necessary by the rise of new cults, the courts would in time build a body of precedent which would be relied on to define what constitutes orthodoxy in America. When that happens—when the political order undertakes to declare what is and what is not religious and to subsidize the orthodoxies which it favors—the state will in fact *be* the church, and civil as well as religious liberty will have to be recovered by the people all over again.

The free exercise of religion, as named in the First Amendment, is closely linked with the provision which prohibits Congress from making laws respecting an establishment of religion. The form under which the greatest pressure is being placed on Congress to violate the establishment clause concerns tax support of religious activities or institutions. The aim of the suppliants may be nothing more than to secure finances for hard-pressed church schools. But the achievement of that aim will inescapably require the organs of government to render judgments infringing on the freedom of religion and to corrupt the proper functioning of the state. It is only when the institutions, including the financial institutions, of church and state are kept scrupulously separated that civil as well as religious liberty is secure.

Rather than allow the corruption of our liberties, we should seek the solutions to our problems in other than constitutional areas. Our serious crises in education—public and parochial—can be dealt with without blurring the distinctions between public and sectarian systems. The differences between the churches, some of which affect church-state relations, afford an opportunity for the constructive dialogue which has already begun in Protestant and Catholic ecumenical movements. The friendly spirit of Pope John XXIII made a significant difference before he convened the Second Vatican Council and an even more important improvement in relations since that time.

Slowly we are beginning to catch up with the insight of the unknown Roman Catholic priest whom Alexis de Tocqueville questioned more than a century ago on a voyage across Lake Michigan to Green Bay: "Do you think that the support of the civil power is useful to religion? A. I am profoundly convinced that it is harmful. . . . All religious beliefs are on the same footing here. The government neither sustains nor persecutes any one; and doubtless there is not a country in the world where the Catholic religion counts adherents more fervent and proselytes more numerous. I repeat, the less religion and its ministers are mixed with civil government, the less part will they take in political dissensions, and the more power religious ideas will gain."[35]

[35] Pierson, Tocqueville and Beaumont in America 298 (1938).

WILLIAM GORMAN

Problems of Church and

State in the United States:

A Catholic View

TOWARD A MORE PERFECT UNION REGARDING THE
AMERICAN CIVIL LIBERTY OF RELIGION*

Everyone is aware of the currently agitated state of several major
issues of policy on the relations of the government and the churches
in our society. The principle that must preside over deliberation
about such issues of policy is the principle of religious liberty. The
suggestion of this article is that what I call the "state of the principle," which I take to be bad, is the cause of our troubles about
the issues of policy.

The principle of religious liberty is a principle of jurisprudence.
As such, it has a somewhat separate, purely intellectual existence
wherever in the republic of letters jurisprudence is being taught,
written, and read. But with us, it is also a constitutional principle.
As such, it is supposed to contribute to our very being and unity

WILLIAM GORMAN is a staff member of the Center for the Study of
Democratic Institutions.

* The excessive pomp in this title came from two circumstances. One was
that coarse saying: "With the ACLU for a friend, religious liberty doesn't
need an enemy." The other was a vague discontent with my Conference bill-
ing, "A Catholic View," since, though a Catholic viewer, what I am looking
at, or for, is the structure and content of our constitutional consensus sign-
able, so to speak, by all members of our body politic.

as a people, to regulate our effort throughout both society and government to be prudent, or practically wise, about certain issues of justice.

The state of the principle, then, would be a function of its many-dimensioned existence. A judgment about the state of the principle would be a judgment of the quality and confluent relations of the people's understanding, moral customs, and emotions in this sphere, of the actions taken and reasons given by legislatures and courts on problems posed to government from society, and of the discussion in the schools of law.

Surely, when the "state of the principle" is understood in that appropriately complex way, no one disputes that it has been bad. In the fifteen years from *Everson* to *Engel*,[1] the relations between the people, their government, and the jurisprudents have been seriously incoherent.

That is not good for life in our time. But it matters in a broader historical perspective. The American approach to church-state problems as old as human history has yielded, despite bad episodes, one of the major social and political achievements of modern times. The full import of our experience could be held back from human history by a prolonged period of incoherent squabbling. It would be something "too bad" if this should happen.

In this short paper I shall submit the somewhat peremptory judgment that there have all along been deficiencies in our doctrine of religious liberty that must now be remedied. To give shape to that judgment I intend, first, to locate two places of weakness by means of a somewhat *ad hoc* hypothesis about doctrinal development and, second, to indicate, in ten points, the weaknesses I seem to see in those two places.

I

My hypothesis about the doctrinal development can be indicated by altering Figgis' famous dictum to read: Religious liberty in America is the residuary legatee of ecclesiastical animosities and

[1] Everson v. Board of Education, 330 U.S. 1 (1947) ; Engel v. Vitale, 370 U.S. 421 (1962).

of the Enlightenment's animosity toward all ecclesiasticism. That
is to say, the state of mind at the moment of constitutional commitment was a complex function of two things: first, the experiences
and determinations of the several free and dissenting churches and,
second, the convictions and aspirations of the sectarian Enlightened
Deists. One group, after experiences of persecution and of civil
disfavor, wanted freedom *from* the state *for* religious communities.
The other group, really wishing a pox on all the religious houses,
wanted freedom *from* religion *for* the political community. The
first wanted no intrusion of civil authority or power into the religious realm; the second wanted no intrusion of religious authority
or power into the political realm. The first wanted politics not to
corrupt religion; the second wanted religion not to corrupt politics.
Since I think it fair to think of Enlightenment Deism as a sort of
unreligion, the second group wanted freedom *from* religion *for*
the unreligious in their conduct of the civil community.

The solution that has developed seems neat enough. The Constitution's religion article, the first sixteen words of the First Amendment, has two grammatically co-ordinate parts. And they are assigned to do duty for the two vectors of desire of the two groups.
Whatever it may have meant at the beginning,[2] the first part, under
constitutional development, holds the desire of the second group.
"Congress shall make no law respecting an establishment of religion" means that there will be freedom from religion for government, because government is constitutionally not allowed to have
anything to do with or for religion. The second part, which adds
that Congress shall make no law "prohibiting the free exercise
thereof," serves the desire of the first group.

Thus interpreted, the two-part religion article is not a statement
of the constitutional principle of religious liberty; it is a statement
of an attempt at constitutional resolution of the problem of the
relations between churches and the state.

---

[2] The argument about original meaning probably has no practical importance. The most luminous demonstration about the letter of the law written
in Philadelphia will not move those who are convinced that its spirit, in any
case, was pure Virginian.

Any bright schoolboy taking, so to speak, just an algebraic look, might well exclaim: "What's the difficulty? The two vectors of desire have their arrows pointed directly away from one another. Both groups want two enterprises *separated*. They are to be separated. Isn't everyone happy?"

The schoolboy's quick sense of the matter is certainly popular and dominant. Indeed, as everyone knows, the actual words of the Constitution are usually bypassed. In popular discussion, in the press, and even in court opinions, they are replaced by the phrase, "the American principle of *separation* of church and state." (And "separation means separation, not something less,"[3] Justice Frankfurter once said, as though talking to Alice.) When there is need for a special show of feeling, the phrase is "the *wall of separation* between church and state."

The history of that ugly metaphor tells my story. First used by Roger Williams, a sort of patron saint for those who fear corruption of religion from any touch of politics, the metaphor was repeated by Thomas Jefferson, patron saint for modern sectarian liberals who fear corruption of politics from any touch of religion. The point is that these two, from entirely opposed positions about religion, agreed wholeheartedly on "the wall of separation." And their direct followers are presently the most busy at masonry. It is a strange alliance, even though they of course do guard duty on opposite sides of the wall.

Two points, then, emerge from my heuristic hypothesis:

1) The religion clause in the First Amendment is not to be merely the religious-liberty clause. The clause is to cover also the freedom of irreligion—freedom from religion for the unreligious.

2) It being granted by all that the religious associations and the political association are distinct, the problem of what relations should obtain between them is to be settled by the concept of separation.

The whole clause, in its current interpretation, translates

[3] McCollum v. Board of Education, 333 U.S. 203, 231 (1948) (opinion of Frankfurter, J.).

not at all badly into a simple formula: *Congress and the state legislatures must neither help nor harm religion.*

No one quarrels about the second part—no harm. (Attempts at the political extirpation of religion are left to other lands.) But there is very deep division of feeling about the first part—no help. On the one hand, there are, as the saying goes, "those who" are vehemently content with "no help to religion." They divide roughly into three groups:

1) Some Christian religious communities, because they hold, on religious grounds, that help from a political source could not be help but would have to be harm.

2) Most Judaic communities, because they think that efforts at non-discriminating help could not turn out to be really non-discriminating as between the many Christian communities and the Jewish communities.

3) Most, if not all, non-religious citizens, because they think an agreement on no harm balanced by an agreement on no help quite fair and a good juridical embodiment of what they consider the higher presiding principle, freedom of conscience.

On the other hand, there are those who are dismayed, indeed flabbergasted, at how the "neither help nor harm" formula seems to be working out. This group includes most in my religious community, most in several different Protestant communities, some in a few Jewish communities, and a few, perhaps, in no religious community. The expressions from this side are usually exclamatory:

The masons standing guard by that quixotic wall are a sort of un-church militant, fighting in a cold civil war for control of society, culture, and government!

We are being outmaneuvered by this strange alliance of militant secularists, simplistic Christians, and too-insecure non-Christians!

The principle of abolute separation is some sort of fraud, hostile to religious liberty!

Absolutely-no-help hurts and, therefore, violates the principle of absolutely-no-harm!

Roughly, that appears to be the social state of the principle—a conflict between those vehemently contented with the present operative interpretation and those violently amazed about where that interpretation seems to lead.

But that is not all. Certainly one can detect a widespread tendency to consign the whole problem to social physics: to assume that this whole matter is inherently and inevitably conflictful; that no genuine consensus can preside at the level of principle over expectable conflicts regarding policies; that the courts can only somehow absorb or somehow smother the divisive group feelings.

My political philosophy compels me to concern about any such capitulation to social physics. The abdication of hope for reason and for consensus at the level of constitutional principle would be a very grave disease in the body politic. In the hope of warding off such a disease, we ought to take the present social situation as possibly signaling deficiencies and inadequacies in our constitutional doctrine.

II

My telescopic account of the development of the religious-liberty doctrine has emphasized two things about it: (1) The religion clause is asked to do service for two different desires, two different freedoms—a freedom for religion and a freedom from religion for irreligion. (2) In consequence, the right relations between the religious associations and the political association are supposed to be comprehended under the concept of "separation."

I now propose to submit five points to indicate difficulties I have with the first aspect of the doctrine and five points to indicate difficulties I have with the second aspect. My intention for the ten points is really in the interrogative mood, but I venture to pose them declaratively.

First.—Religious liberty is already infringed by the rationale that makes the religion clause do simultaneous duty for the freedoms of religion and of irreligion.

Religion, at least as understood in the major Biblical churches, is gravely misunderstood when it is thought that religious liberty and liberty of irreligion are somehow co-ordinate species under a generic, superior liberty of thought or of conscience. To be sure, acts of faith and of religion are not truly such unless they are interiorly free acts. But the existence of a religion is not constituted by the individual subjective conscience projecting from itself demands it freely wills to place upon itself. In the traditional Biblical religions absolute authority does not lie with the individual conscience but with God. A religion exists after the Divine entrance into history and from the encounter of the conscience with imperatives divinely projected into history and transmitted as something objective by the instrumental authority of a tradition and a church.

For a life responsive to imperatives freely believed to be objective and Divine, the assertion of a right to religious liberty is not an assertion of something that is one species of the right to freedom of conscience. Constitutional interpretation "establishing" a mistake about religion presents the unfunny comedy of a violation of religious liberty within the constitutional article that institutes religious liberty.

Second.—No such mistake need have been made or need be continued in our constitutional history, because the clauses following the religion clause impart constitutional status to the freedom of irreligion in a positive and proper way.

The freedoms of thought, of conscience, and of the academy are effectuated, both logically and in our constitutional development, by the freedoms of speech, of press, and of assembly and by Article VI of the Constitution, which bans any religious test for office. Could a case be made that something rightfully claimable for irreligion is not comprehended in such guarantees? If not, what is the point of twisting the non-establishment part of the religion clause into an additional protection for irreligion?

Third.—If the religion clause were construed as not including the freedom of irreligion, since it is protected elsewhere, then no special inhibition would attach to government regarding actions taken to secure the blessing of religious liberty; and certain problems of social policy could then be clearly seen as involving the need to balance the concurrent claims of several important constitutional liberties.

In the complex, contingent affairs of a society whose citizens belong respectively to many churches and to no church, it is to be expected that conflicts will occur about ways of securing the several First Amendment liberties.

The effort at orderly resolution of those conflicts must balance the concurrent claims of all the rights involved. But in such an effort, concern for religious liberty cannot rightly be inhibited by a sort of operative a priori, enjoying constitutional status, that concern for religious liberty would automatically entail unconstitutional consequences for other liberties.

It is hardly possible not to note that most of those who applaud the current "absolutist" interpretation of the secular First Amendment freedoms also applaud the interpretation of the religion clause that places an absolutely inherent limitation, for irreligion's sake, on what can be done to secure religious liberty. Such an observation ought to be cautionary against smugness about devotion to civil liberties. It is always widely suspected that religious people cannot add to their concern for religious liberty due concern for other valid liberties. Whatever the basis for such a suspicion in the American scene, certainly it is clear that partiality in one's devotion to all valid civil liberties is something imperfect, whatever the direction of one's partiality. The great promise in the American scene lies precisely in the fund of good will that exists about the importance of achieving a justly balanced devotion to all our constitutional liberties. It might be salutary to proclaim a moratorium on smugness, from any side, about the completeness of one's devotion to civil liberties.

Fourth.—Constitutional interpretation should construe the second part of the religion clause as proscribing the "abridgment" of the free exercise of religion.

Such an amendment in understanding and operative interpretation would be a further step toward bringing religious liberty into constitutional parity with the other liberties and toward underlining the point about balancing liberties. "Abridging," not "prohibiting," is the term used for the other First Amendment liberties.

Such an amendment would permit rational discussion of claims by religious citizens that certain actions of Congress would, unless the exigencies of religious liberty are brought into balance, not so much "prohibit" as "abridge" their religious liberty.

Fifth.—Actions taken by Congress or by state legislatures to secure, or avoid the abridgment of, religious liberty cannot in reason be construed as actions "aiding," or "establishing," religion.

There are good reasons why a free pluralist society should have a perduring "prepossession" against direct governmental aid to religion. These good reasons would reflect a concern for the right understanding of religion, for the security of religious liberty, for a good balance of all natural liberties, for the autonomy of the civil order, and for the right mode of relation for churches to government. In my judgment, then, an operative consensus against direct governmental aid to religion should be a part of our constitutional tradition.

However, only from weakness of mind or malice of will could such a consensus against direct aid to religion be construed as preventing governmental action to avoid abridgments of religious liberty. One instance of what I take to be at stake in this point is the issue of governmental aid to parochial schools, a major issue of policy currently in an agitated state. I have discussed this subject at length in a paper[4] that concludes with the contention that our sound "prepossession" against direct aid to religion is currently preventing us from sensing the unjust abridgment of religious liberty that lies in the burden currently placed upon some religious parents when they wish to make a choice regarding the education of their children.

To be sure, governmental action taken to avoid abridgment of religious liberty would *indirectly* entail "aid to religion." And, to be sure, the distinction between direct aid to religion and indirect aid resulting from concern for religious liberty might, in the first instance, be something too subtle for the understanding of "ordinary people." But surely it is precisely the function of the legal art, as exercised by judges and by jurisprudents in the schools of law,

[4] Gorman, *A Case of Distributive Justice,* in RELIGION AND THE SCHOOLS 34 (The Fund for the Republic 1959).

to make and then effectively teach whatever subtle distinctions the doing of justice requires.

A summation of my first five points would be the contention that constitutional interpretation ought not to obfuscate in order to create an invalid imparity for religious liberty.

Sixth.—A constitutional consensus about right relations between the two associations cannot be taken as implying a sort of code of specifications for the political "orthodoxy" of churches, involving tenets, structure, and procedures to which churches must conform so as to be consonant with the democratic enterprise.

On the contrary, religious liberty exacts the privilege of self-definition for churches.

Seventh.—A constitutional consensus about right relations cannot be taken as implying that all who consent have reached the point of consent by some one "right" way of inference.

On the contrary, religious liberty exacts the privilege for churches of developing, from their own self-understanding, their own routes to consent about right relations.

I submit that the denial of these last two points has widespread social existence. The genuineness and vitality of our consensus are certainly diminished by what might be called "suspicion with constitutional intensity."

In its crudest form, the suspicion takes something like the following form. If there is a church in our society that does not have enough sacral feeling about the democratic enterprise to democratize itself, then it is somehow disloyal at the very constitutional level, and the genuineness of its consent can be doubted, since its "authoritarian" structure deprives it of any sound route toward consent.

It is easily within anyone's memory that civil libertarians and fraternal Protestants have not leaped to rebuke even the crudest publications of this "suspicion." There may have been good reason for such hesitancy. Perhaps the suspicion, if uncrudely formulated, has historical justification.

Certainly it is true that the Roman Catholic Church, even in America, stubbornly refuses to be, even to a degree, *latitudinarian* regarding its claim to religious truth, *congregationalist* in its ecclesiastical polity, or *collegialist* regarding its status in society as just one of the many sorts of infra-political associations composing society.

Does such a fact, thus posed in uncrude, old-fashioned technical terms, mean that the Catholic Church must perforce have secret reservations about a constitutional consensus that involves its members with members of other churches and of no church? It is permissible for me to think, as I do, that the fact need not have any such implication and that my church has not as yet been brilliantly persuasive on the point. Perhaps it is a case of suspicion breeding suspense.

Pending further developments, however, it occurs to me to underline my sixth and seventh points by a reminder about the logic of the hypothetical syllogism. In any elementary textbook, the following truths are set forth. Valid inference: If P, then Q; but P, therefore Q. Invalid inference (fallacy of denying the antecedent) : If P, then Q; but not-P, therefore not-Q. Invalid inference (fallacy of affirming the consequent) : If P, then Q; but Q, therefore P.

If the constitutional consensus in a society philosophically and religiously pluralist is to be genuine, then these two fallacies must be avoided. There must, that is, be a clear socio-political realization that there is no one right route to consent, and that the fact of consent does not imply that some one right route has been taken.

Eighth.—A constitutional consensus about right relations does imply the binding consequence that the autonomy of the civil order must be respected.

The condition precedent to the institution of religious liberty has been the assertion of a distinction, a radical duality, between religious associations and the political association. This distinction, firmly inserted in history by Christianity, surely implies that there is to be for each of the associations a kind of autonomy.

From the assertion of radical duality there is a binding consequence against "clericalism," if that term can be used to stand for actions that tend to violate the autonomy of the civil order, actions that strive to make it purely instrumental to the purposes of a religious association.

Ninth.—However, the binding consequence regarding respect for civil autonomy does not entail an agreement that religion has no concern about the public domain and can seek no influence therein.

The distinction that is the basis of the obligation to respect civil autonomy is not a distinction between associations of the same order, but a distinction between associations of entirely different orders. It is the radical discontinuity in type that allows religious associations to strive for an influence on the civil order which, because conformed to their type, does not violate the autonomy of the civil order.

Certainly it has to be noted that in more than one of the traditional Biblical churches it is an article of religious belief that influence in the civil order must be striven for. A proscription against such an effort, made either in constitutional interpretation or in social custom, would be, to such churches, a violation of the principle of religious liberty.

The whole point about right relations between churches and the state is a *modal* point. In a democracy—the best and only truly just form of government—religious influence in the civil order, when proper in mode, will be mediated through the consciences of members of churches and will take effect through their activity, as members of the political association, in accord with just constitutional requirements for the political process.

Perhaps my eighth and ninth points should be summed up in a sort of riddle:

> For Politics to be
> in Due Autonomy
> it need not be the case
> that Religion is a mere Private Place
> with no relation to *Publica Res.*

Finally.—A political "people" from its right to autonomy in the temporal sphere can rightfully resist "clericalism" and rightfully through its government restrict religious influence improper in mode.

Actions taken to protect the formal secularity of social and political prudence do not violate religious liberty. They instruct it.

The American political people, whatever its present difficulties regarding issues of policy, is deeply committed to the continuing search for a mature prudence about the right relations between religious associations and the political association. In our context, the most effective resistance to violations of civil autonomy by immature religious associations would probably come from members of those associations who are sensitive about their concurrent membership in the political association.

Contrary to what many think, citizens who are members of religious associations need not be less sensitive to political freedom as a human perfection than are citizens who belong only to the political association.

III

Before releasing my ten points for your consideration, perhaps I can be allowed some comment on them. With the first five points I am trying, at a minimum, to suggest that there are serious questions that can be raised about the current constitutional understanding and position of the right to religious liberty. With the other five points I am trying, at a minimum, to suggest that important points about due autonomy and modally right relations cannot be attained within the too crude concept of "separation." In general, I am asserting that our constitutional doctrine has deficiencies that hurt civic friendship and aggravate conflicts about just policies.

If you disagree with all ten points but do agree that they are not merely polemical or "interested" points and thus deserve to be controverted, then you agree with the one point of which I am sure. I am sure, that is, that we need a work in jurisprudence, critically detached from recent confusion in the Supreme Court, a work that would indeed advance us toward a more perfect union regarding the American civil liberty of religion.

For that needed work in jurisprudence I would like to submit a motto. It is from Lord Acton, a "Catholic viewer" with a deep concern for political liberty. It reads as follows: "Civil and religious liberty are so commonly associated in people's mouths, and are so rare in fact, that their definition is evidently as little understood as the principle of their connection. The point at which they unite, the common root from which they derive their sustenance, is the right of self-government."[5]

[5] ACTON, ESSAYS ON FREEDOM AND POWER 89 (1948).

ROBERT F. DRINAN

The Constitutionality
of Public Aid to
Parochial Schools

It would be an easy answer to the question under discussion in this paper if we could simply state that no public funds should ever be expended for private purposes. With regard to schools, however, the fact is that no non-public school can ever be private in every sense of that term. In *Pierce v. Society of Sisters*[1] the United States Supreme Court recognized the right of the private school to exist as a substitute for the public school, thereby giving private schools a juridical status. This status, however ambiguous, has rendered the private or parochial school a quasi-public or, if you will, a "para-public" institution.

The fundamental issue in the controversy over public funds for private schools, including parochial schools, therefore arises out of the fact that private schools are public schools for the purpose of compulsory attendance laws, but have not been designated as public schools capable of being the beneficiaries of public funds. The anomalous juridical status of the private school in America has no parallel or precedent in any other phase of our law. Those who seek

ROBERT F. DRINAN, S.J., is Dean and Professor of Law, Boston College Law School.

[1] 268 U.S. 510 (1925).

to retain *Pierce* and yet reverse *Everson v. Board of Education*[2] do not appreciate the implications of the juridical position conferred on the private school by *Pierce*. Those who seek to retain *Pierce* and who would accept *Everson* as containing the ultimate concessions which can be made to the private school likewise do not appreciate the logical implications of the holding in *Pierce*.

THE PUBLIC DIMENSIONS OF PRIVATE SCHOOLS

Let us start then with *Pierce* and see if from this decision there can be developed a line of reasoning by which the private school can claim to be an institution charged with a public responsibility and hence eligible for some public funds.

As is well known, *Pierce* was decided a few days before the guarantees of the First Amendment were for the first time recognized to be applicable to the states via the Fourteenth Amendment.[3] Consequently, *Pierce* decided nothing about First Amendment freedoms in relation to the existence of the private school. But the spirit of the *Pierce* decision clearly affirmed that no institutionalized dissent from educational orthodoxy could be constitutionally suppressed. The brief opinion in *Pierce*, however, left almost totally unsolved the extent to which a private school, legally recognized as a permissible substitute for the public school, could on this basis claim a right to be supported by public funds.

A plausible argument can be made for the proposition that the *Pierce* decision elevated the private school to the status of a publicly recognized institution which cannot logically and fairly be granted state accreditation and denied state subsidization. Even if everyone agreed with this conclusion, however, the real issue confronting the nation today would not be resolved. That issue is, of course, not the private school as private, but the church-related school and, more particularly, the Catholic school.

In order, therefore, to give reality to the discussion, it is proposed to talk here not in a conceptualistic way about public money and private schools but in a realistic way about federal aid and

2 330 U.S. 1 (1947).

3 Gitlow v. New York, 268 U.S. 652 (1925).

Catholic educational institutions. At the same time it must be recognized that no satisfactory resolution of the controversy over the very small subsidy to church-related schools which is in issue in connection with federal aid can be reached without attaining some agreement on the function and juridical nature of the private school in America.

What then is the claim being made by Catholic parents and Catholic officials? The claim is a very small one: the Catholic contention is that, *if* federal aid is to be enacted, *some* recognition should be given to Catholic schools. This Catholic request is grounded on several factors among which are the following: (1) About 92 per cent of all children attending private schools in America today are enrolled in Catholic elementary and secondary schools. (2) Some six million students—or every eighth child in America—attend Catholic schools. Any program designed to elevate the nation's standards of educational excellence which ignores the 12 per cent of the nation's school children enrolled in non-public schools is seriously neglecting a significant element in the population. (3) The first program of massive federal aid to education must be designed either to help public schools alone or to elevate the educational excellence of *all* schools. Consequently, an important public-policy decision must be made before federal aid can become a reality.

Even this telescoped version of the Catholic case for a share in the distribution of federal aid to education will indicate that the controversy over this issue involves profound questions of public policy. These questions can be resolved in a speculative way by peering into the interstices of the half dozen church-state opinions which the Supreme Court has written from *Everson* to *Engel v. Vitale*.[4] But even the most resourceful and convinced advocate or opponent of federal aid for Catholic schools must confess that the most careful reading of all Supreme Court decisions and dicta leads only to the feeling that the real questions have not yet been asked, much less resolved, in Supreme Court jurisprudence.

Some few "absolutes," however, with regard to religion and

[4] 370 U.S. 421 (1962).

education have emerged from the line of cases from *Everson* to *Engel*. The following principles seem to have a secure place in church-state law:

I. The benefits of public welfare legislation may not be granted or denied to citizens because of their religious faith or their lack of it.

II. If the state, in the pursuit of a legitimate public purpose, selects means to achieve this purpose which have an incidental effect of assisting religion, such means are not thereby unconstitutional—especially if no alternate means are as easily available.

III. No sectarian teaching or religious practice may be constitutionally permitted on the premises of a tax-supported school —even if student and teacher participation is on a truly voluntary basis.

Analyzing in turn each of these three broad principles, what can one conclude about the constitutionality of a grant of public money to a Catholic school?

I. Public Welfare Legislation

If there was one thing that Mr. Justice Black sought to make clear in *Everson* it was the finding that the challenged statute authorizing reimbursement to Catholic parents for school-bus transportation for their children was public welfare legislation. Mr. Justice Black assumed or asserted several conclusions which formed the following line of reasoning: (1) Public welfare legislation is ordinarily identifiable as a particular type of law and should not be nullified by the courts except for the gravest reasons. (2) Such public welfare legislation is not unconstitutional even if it facilitates attendance at church-related schools. (3) Such legislation does not offend against the wall of separation between church and state provided that (*a*) any aid given to religion is incidental to the main purpose of the law and (*b*) a denial of such aid would be discrimination against persons or groups because of their faith or lack of it.

It may be that someone would challenge the foregoing summary of *Everson* as inadequate and even misleading. Such a person could, indeed, cite respectable authority for his position, because the fact is that several state courts have been confused about the meaning and thrust of *Everson*. The opinion of Mr. Justice Black is more encouraging to the advocate of federal aid for Catholic schools than are the several interpretations placed on the opinion by the four dissenting justices in *Everson*. Equally discouraging are the interpretations given to *Everson* by the supreme courts of the states of Alaska, New Mexico, Oregon, Vermont, Washington, and Wisconsin.[5] All these tribunals have given lip service to *Everson* but have declared laws granting bus transportation or other benefits to Catholic-school children to be unconstitutional even though these laws were concededly written and enacted as public welfare legislation. In other words, state courts have *not* accepted the idea that public welfare legislation is constitutionally permissible if it only grants to children in Catholic schools those benefits which are also granted to pupils in public schools. The basic rationale of *Everson* has either been misunderstood, misinterpreted, or rejected. Only the supreme courts of Connecticut and Maine[6] have accepted and followed *Everson* as meaning that bus-transportation statutes can be framed as public welfare legislation in such a manner as to be constitutionally unassailable.

The confusion over the meaning of *Everson* has not been lessened by the fact that the United States Supreme Court has, since 1951, refused to review decisions based on *Everson* from the states of

[5] Matthews v. Quinton, 362 P.2d 932 (Alaska 1961), *appeal dismissed and cert. denied*, 368 U.S. 517 (1962); Zellers v. Huff, 55 N.M. 501, 236 P.2d 949 (1951); Dickman v. School Dist., 366 P.2d 533 (Ore. 1961), *cert. denied*, 371 U.S. 823 (1962); Swart v. South Burlington Town School Dist., 122 Vt. 177, 167 A.2d 514 (1961), *cert. denied*, 366 U.S. 925 (1961); Visser v. Nooksack Valley School Dist., 33 Wash.2d 699, 207 P.2d 198 (1949); Reynolds v. Nusbaum, 17 Wis.2d 148, 115 N.W.2d 761 (1962); *cf.* McVey v. Hawkins, 364 Mo. 44, 258 S.W.2d 927 (1953).

[6] Snyder v. Town of Newton, 147 Conn. 374, 161 A.2d 770 (1960), *appeal dismissed for want of a substantial federal question*, 365 U.S. 299 (1961); Squires v. City of Augusta, 155 Me. 151, 153 A.2d 80 (1959) (dictum).

Alaska, Connecticut, Oregon, and Vermont.[7] One can argue, therefore, either that *Everson* is properly interpreted by the highest court
of Connecticut, which sustained the constitutionality of a law authorizing bus transportation to private schools, or that *Everson* has
almost no relevance or meaning at the state level, as the highest
courts of Alaska, Oregon, Washington, and Wisconsin have declared.[8]

It will be seen, therefore, that the history of *Everson* does not
encourage one to employ it as a firm foundation for a case for
federal aid to Catholic schools. At the same time, the literal word-
ing of Mr. Justice Black's opinion in *Everson* supplies a solid basis
for a line of argument that would support the case which Catholics
and others are making on behalf of the constitutionality of federal
aid for private schools. The fact is that *Everson* reaffirmed *Cochran
v. Louisiana State Board of Education*[9] and the child-benefit theory
and that *Everson* is still good law—despite *McCollum v. Board of
Education*,[10] *Torcaso v. Watkins*,[11] and *Engel v. Vitale*. Mr. Leo
Pfeffer highlights the consequences of Mr. Justice Black's opinion
in this comment:

> When the Everson decision is coupled with the Cochran decision, they
> lead logically to the conclusion that a state may, notwithstanding the
> First Amendment, finance practically every aspect of parochial educa-
> tion, with the exception of such comparatively minor items as the pro-
> portionate salaries of teachers while they teach the catechism. . . .[12]

One could add a dimension to Mr. Pfeffer's reading of the
Cochran-Everson rule by urging that, in the ultimate analysis,
Everson follows from *Pierce*. Public money, in other words, cannot logically be withheld from the private school if it is publicly
accredited as an institution where children may fulfil their legal
duty to attend school.

The many ambiguities in the *Pierce-Cochran-Everson* line of

[7] Cases cited notes 5 and 6 *supra*.

[8] *Ibid.*

[9] 281 U.S. 370 (1930).

[10] 333 U.S. 203 (1948).

[11] 367 U.S. 488 (1961).

[12] PFEFFER, CHURCH, STATE AND FREEDOM 476 (1953).

cases arise from the enigma which lies behind the institution that has been assigned the non-descriptive and unenlightening name of the non-public or private school. Schools of this kind have an equivocal juridical status in America, and until that status is clarified the entire controversy over the financing of such schools will be carried on in language and with concepts which do not really express the realities which they seek to describe. The terms "private" and "public" become even less useful when the private school in issue turns out to be a church-related school. The thorny issues involved in this area lead us to a discussion of the second "absolute" in the *Everson* to *Engel* line of cases—namely, the proposition that the state may constitutionally achieve a legitimate public purpose in such a way that an unintended, incidental benefit comes to religion.

II. State Programs Which Give Incidental Aid to Religion

The various Supreme Court opinions in the Sunday-law cases made it very clear that the requirement of separation between church and state does not mean that the state, in carrying out a legitimate secular purpose, must do so in a way which gives no aid to religion. It is significant to note that Mr. Justice Black, who wrote the rigorously separationist language in *Everson* and *McCollum*, sees no problem involving establishment or free exercise of religion in Sunday laws which, whatever their present purpose may be said to be, clearly aid the Christian religion by fixing Sunday as a day of universal rest.

It is the *secular* purpose behind Sunday laws which, in the mind of the Supreme Court, renders them constitutional. As Mr. Justice Frankfurter put it in his concurring opinion in the Sunday-law cases: "not every regulation some of whose practical effects may facilitate the observance of a religion by its adherents affronts the requirement of church-state separation."[13]

Employing this reasoning, the majority of the Supreme Court

---

[13] McGowan v. Maryland, 366 U.S. 420, 467 (1961) (opinion of Frankfurter, J.).

held that the incidental aid which Sunday laws give to the Christian religion does not make them unconstitutional. Nor are these laws contrary to the First Amendment because of the "indirect burden on religious observance" which they impose on Sabbatarians. There is, however, a qualification on the power of the state to impose such a burden. As Chief Justice Warren put it:

But if the State regulates conduct by enacting a general law within its power, the purpose and effect of which is to advance the State's secular goals, the statute is valid despite its indirect burden on religious observance *unless the State may accomplish its purpose by means which do not impose such a burden.*[14]

Is it arguable from this principle that the state in carrying out its "secular goals" in the field of education has some obligation to do so, if possible, in a manner which does not impose even an "indirect burden on religious observance"? If Catholics could demonstrate that the denial of aid to their schools imposed a burden on their religious observance, would such a law be subject to the qualification which Chief Justice Warren attached to Sunday laws?

Whatever one might answer to that question, it is clear that the establishment clause has *not* been interpreted by the Supreme Court to mean that the secular aims of the state must be achieved in a manner deliberately designed to preclude any incidental aid to religion. In view of this position, then, what policy can the state adopt with regard to the distribution of funds for the purpose of raising the nation's standards of excellence in education?

The advocates of federal aid for Catholic schools ground their plea on the principle that the state, in carrying out its secular goals in the field of education, can comply with the First Amendment if it makes available funds for strictly secular purposes in *all* schools. Under such an arrangement no aid is intended for religion, and whatever benefits students in church-related schools may receive are exclusively of a secular nature.

The two most fundamental objections to this line of reasoning are the following:

[14] Braunfeld v. Brown, 366 U.S. 599, 607 (1961) (opinion of Warren, C.J.). (Emphasis added.)

1. Even if public money were given to a Catholic school for strictly secular objectives, these objectives would be carried forward in an atmosphere permeated by a Catholic orientation.

2. Even if this permeation can be prevented, the grant of public money to a Catholic school makes available to this school funds which would otherwise be committed to the teaching of secular subjects.

Let us try to analyze and, if possible, bring some clarification to these two issues.

The permeation argument against aid to Catholic schools does not contend that the legitimate secular purpose which the state seeks to fulfil in giving aid for education in secular subjects is thwarted or frustrated in Catholic schools. The secular purpose is concededly carried out in Catholic schools, but it is permeated—and somehow constitutionally contaminated—by a sectarian atmosphere. The argument against aid to church-related schools because of the permeation of sacred or sectarian values into the teaching of secular subjects must assume for its validity the viewpoint that the state is constitutionally required to seek ways to carry out its secular objectives which will not give even incidental aid to religion. No such constitutional requirement can be found in the decisions from *Everson* to *Engel,* and indeed the opinions in the Sunday-law cases expressly deny the existence of any such constitutional requirement.

The opponents of federal aid for Catholic schools who place great reliance on the permeation argument must logically say that the secular or silent attitude with regard to religion in the public schools is the only official orthodoxy which the state is allowed to promote in the pursuance of its public welfare objectives. This may be a philosophy of education subscribed to by a majority of the American people, but it is not good constitutional law nor, it is submitted, sound public policy.

Some recent writings on the permeation issue have focused attention on some graphic examples of the intermingling, or rather, the intrusion, of sectarian teaching into textbooks on secular sub-

jects used in Catholic schools. Two comments on this matter seem
appropriate.

First, no scientific study has ever been done on the extent of the
permeation of sectarian teaching in the instruction in secular subjects in Catholic schools. Concrete examples of such permeation
in textbooks can be cited, but an important distinction should be
made between the factitious and indefensible insertion of sectarian
symbols or teaching into secular subjects and the conclusions or
judgments based on religious values which are properly found in
texts in the area of the social sciences. The latter type of permeation is much more significant than the former and is, moreover,
a justifiable exercise of academic freedom by social scientists
writing from a particular point of view.

Second, although there undoubtedly exist some unjustifiable
examples of permeation in secular textbooks used in Catholic
schools, little work has been done on the extent to which ultra-
nationalistic or secularistic symbols and teachings have permeated
the textbooks used in the public schools of America. Studies have
shown, however, that the beliefs of minority groups, religious influences in American history, and the religions of lands different
from America have received very inadequate treatment in the textbooks which enjoy widespread use in the nation's public schools.
Many of these texts can be fairly and properly criticized as being
permeated with an excessive emphasis on the secular, with a resulting failure to give adequate treatment to the sacred, the sectarian,
or the spiritual elements in the life of man and of society.

Permeation is therefore a factor in every textbook, since values
are omnipresent. If the state therefore cannot constitutionally give
public money for instruction in secular subjects if religious values
are commingled in the instruction, the state is equally disabled
from financing instruction in secular subjects where the orientation
of the instruction is, by silence or by implication, permeated with
a secularistic outlook.

Those who argue against federal aid for Catholic schools because there exists in these schools some permeation of secular subjects with sacred values must be prepared to accept the major

premise of their argument—the assumption that the orientation of secular humanism is the only type of educational orthodoxy which the state can subsidize.

Even if permeation of secular instruction with sectarian teaching can be prevented, however, the additional argument is made that the granting of public money to non-public schools for instruction in secular subjects relieves this school from a financial obligation which it would otherwise have. Hence a church-related school would have more funds available to it, and such funds could be used for sectarian purposes.

The logical thrust of this argument leads to the conclusion that any church-related school must be placed not in the category of a school but of a church. To deny public funds to non-public schools for secular instruction because such a grant would bring to the church-related school a freeing of otherwise committed funds is to state that the fully accredited school which is affiliated with a church thereby loses its right to any public funds even for exclusively secular purposes. Such a conclusion is specifically contrary to the *Everson* decision, where Mr. Justice Black in effect conceded that the public money granted to parents for bus transportation of their children to a Catholic school would make available to the parents and to the school more money for other purposes.

The contention that the state should refuse public funds for the attainment of a secular purpose unrelated to the religious function of a church-related school simply because such a grant would free the funds of this school for a religious purpose leads logically to the conclusion that no church-related institution may be entrusted with the implementation of any of the secular objectives of the state. Such a conclusion runs contrary to the basic traditions and the widespread contemporary practice of the state's assisting church-related social welfare agencies in caring for the sick, the aged, and those in need of social services.

It should be remembered that *Everson* sustained the constitutionality of a law which granted the benefits of public welfare legislation to individuals even though such benefits helped them to get to a church-related school. This result was reached in an opinion in which Mr. Justice Black stated:

No tax in any amount, large or small, can be levied to support any religious activities or institutions, whatever they may be called, or whatever form they may adopt, to teach or practice religion.[15]

This famous sentence proscribes tax support *only* for "*religious* activities or institutions" in whatever form they may adopt "to teach or practice *religion.*" It does *not* proscribe public funds for instruction in secular subjects even though such instruction may be conducted under the auspices of a religious institution. Far less does it forbid the granting of public funds to a church-related institution for the accomplishment of a secular purpose simply because such a grant might liberate other funds of this institution for a religious purpose.

Aid to religion as such is clearly forbidden by all the decisions from *Everson* to *Engel.* But state aid for the improvement of secular education need not be distributed only under circumstances where not even any incidental aid to religion may occur. The broadening of the concept of separation of church and state to this point must necessarily assume the validity of the theory that America is a completely secular state. Such a viewpoint makes it difficult, if not impossible, to reconcile the mandate of the establishment clause with the guarantee of the free-exercise-of-religion clause.

It must be noted, however, that Supreme Court opinions from *Everson* to *Engel* are ambiguous at best with regard to the central question of whether America is a completely secular state. No decision has repudiated Mr. Justice Douglas' assertion in *Zorach v. Clauson*[16] that "we are a religious people whose institutions presuppose a Supreme Being." But in the very same opinion Mr. Justice Douglas wrote that "Government may not . . . blend secular and sectarian education. . . ."[17] The Court has seemingly supported a theistic basis for America's legal institutions but has simultane-

[15] 330 U.S. at 16.

[16] 343 U.S. 306, 313 (1952).   [17] *Id.* at 314.

ously insisted that the public school may not blend any "sectarian education" into its program. This apparent paradox leads us to a consideration of our third "absolute" in church-state law—the unconstitutionality of religious teaching or practices in the public schools, even when they are conducted on a truly voluntary basis.

III. THE SECULAR ORIENTATION OF THE PUBLIC SCHOOL

Mr. Justice Rutledge, dissenting in *Everson*, gave, as a reason for the *Pierce* decision, his conviction that children should not be required to attend public schools because "their atmosphere is *wholly secular*."[18] While it would be difficult to prove or disprove that the Supreme Court has agreed that the public school must have an "atmosphere" that is "wholly secular," the Court would seem to be pointing in that direction.

If the Supreme Court in its present term declares the reading of the Bible and the recitation of the Lord's Prayer in a public school to be unconstitutional, the secularization of the public school will be, at least in popular opinion, considerably extended. In a certain sense, however, the reasoning of the Court in the Bible-reading case will be more important than the result reached. The Court can develop a line of reasoning employed in the past and forbid Bible-reading as contrary to the establishment clause—even if no infringement of religious liberty is found to be present. The Court seems to have followed this reasoning in the *Engel* decision, although the fact of state authorship of the prayer involved in that case made the Court's decision unique.

Very few scholars and no group of religionists have sought to explore the implications of the Supreme Court's recently developed interpretation of the establishment clause as constituting a source of rights independent of the free-exercise-of-religion clause. The theory that the establishment clause is merely instrumental to the implementation of the free-exercise clause has been rejected by the Court. By this rejection the Court has opened up the following questions relating to the constitutionality of aid for private schools.

[18] 330 U.S. at 59. (Emphasis supplied.)

1. Can religionists claim that the secularized public school violates the establishment clause because it prefers irreligion over religion?

2. Can religionists claim further that the state, by assisting only the secularized school, subscribes to and promotes an orthodoxy which is imposed on all students to whom, by law, the state has given a pledge of a free education unaffected by any officially established indoctrination?

Let us search through these ideas in the light of the recent Supreme Court interpretation of the establishment clause.

SECULARIZED SCHOOLS AND THE ESTABLISHMENT CLAUSE

The theory advanced by Mr. Justice Black in *Torcaso, McGowan,* and *Engel*—that the establishment clause can be violated without a violation of the free-exercise-of-religion clause—may now have become an accepted part of Supreme Court jurisprudence. Under this interpretation of the First Amendment can it be argued that the secularization of the public school amounts to a violation of the establishment clause since a particular form of religion (or irreligion) is given a preferential status? If such a violation of the establishment clause can be shown, Catholics or others can enjoin it, even though there is no infringement of anyone's religious freedom.

Aside from the question of standing to sue, can religious parents prove a violation of the establishment clause if the state gives financial assistance only to the school where education is deliberately divorced from religion? Preferential treatment of irreligion would seem to be as constitutionally objectionable as any preference given to religion.

Some Catholics have asserted that attendance at a public school by their children violates or restricts the religious freedom of both children and parents. The assertion is made that Catholics have a right to be treated like conscientious objectors or like Jehovah's Witnesses, who have been granted an exemption from laws requiring a flag salute in a public school.

Mr. Justice Frankfurter saw the force of this analogy when,

dissenting in *West Virginia State Board of Education v. Barnette*,[19] he voted against granting an exemption from the flag salute to children conscientiously opposed to the practice. Mr. Justice Frankfurter saw the consequences of the Court's bowing to the religious scruples of a minority and raised this question: "What of the claims for equality of treatment of those parents who, because of *religious scruples, cannot* send their children to public schools?"[20] This potential argument of the Catholic or other parent has not been developed or litigated. To be able to show that religious parents, "because of religious scruples, cannot send their children to public schools" (to use Mr. Justice Frankfurter's language) would seem to require more proof of an anti-religious bias in the public school than would appear to be now provable.

It is not now necessary, however, to have such proof before one can claim rights by reason of the First Amendment. Under the interpretation of the establishment clause adopted in recent years by the Supreme Court, any preferential treatment granted by the state to religion or irreligion constitutes a violation of constitutional rights. The allegation that is difficult to prove is, of course, the assertion that the secularized public school gives preferential treatment to irreligion. The widespread and deeply held conviction persists that silence about religion in the public school is the same as neutrality or impartiality. On this basic conception is built the whole thesis that the public school can be fair to believers and nonbelievers by assuming that their differences for the purposes of education are without significance. It is this basic assumption of the public school which, it is submitted, violates the letter and the spirit of the establishment clause.

The secularized public school meets and treats its students only as future citizens. Their religious or spiritual beliefs are to be regarded as irrelevant and hence unimportant with respect to the entire educational process. It is this basic disregard of the great ideas and religious aspirations in the lives of the students in a public school which is the gravamen of the religionist's complaint. To the believer—at least to many believers—the silent assumption

[19] 319 U.S. 624 (1943).   [20] *Id.* at 660. (Emphasis supplied.)

by the public school that religion in any meaningful sense is irrelevant to the educational process amounts to an official establishment of secular values.

Two of the greatest ideas underlying American democracy were born in the mid-nineteenth century: the pledge of the state to give a *free* education to every child in an atmosphere not affected by a sectarian orientation. When these twin ideals emerged more than a century ago their fulfilment was relatively easy in a pan-Protestant nation. Today, however, in a religiously pluralistic society these ideals have become more difficult to realize, because the non-denominational pan-Protestant environment of the common school has been largely displaced by a secularistic orientation. The tendency of the law from *Everson* to *Engel* has been to make mandatory the secularization of the public school without at the same time providing for a *free* education in a school without a secularistic orientation.

The denial of public funds to church-related schools means in effect that the ideal of a *free* education in an atmosphere apart from any officially fixed indoctrination has been compromised. The important thing here to prove, of course, is that there is a secularistic indoctrination which accompanies an education in the public school. This is the most important and the most difficult point of dispute in the entire controversy over public funds for private schools. But in a nation whose law knows no heresy and whose legal institutions support no orthodoxy, how is it possible to reject the contention made by a substantial minority of citizens that the tax-supported school, by its silent disregard of religion, thereby promotes irreligion? This, of course, is the essence of the Catholic parent's case, and no satisfactory answer seems to have been given.

It is uncertain what American law would say if tomorrow all the Catholics of the nation withdrew all their children from the public schools because of their conviction that the secularistic orientation of these schools was destructive of the faith of their children.

American courts could compel the children to return to the public schools or could give financing for schools consistent with the consciences of Catholics.

American law today confronts the situation where about half of all the Catholic children of the nation have withdrawn from the public school because of a profound disagreement with the approach to education and to life which that institution has adopted. American society and American law do not seem concerned that these children who, for compelling religious reasons, have forfeited the education offered to them must be thereby deprived of their right to share in the commitment of the state to provide a free education for every future citizen.

Summary and Conclusions

It seems clear that many converging forces have precipitated the national debate about the advisability of parochial schools' sharing in some part of federal aid to education if such assistance is authorized by the Congress. The debate is filled with anomalies, the most curious of which is the fact that almost no controversy exists at the state level over parochial schools, since at that level the question was resolved in the last century when virtually all states enacted laws prohibiting the distribution of public funds to sectarian schools. In the federal-aid controversy Catholic spokesmen are in effect asserting that this policy embraced in the last century by the states is not a wise or fair one for the federal government to follow.

Cogent arguments exist to support the Catholic contention. Among them are the following:

1. The fully accredited private school has important public dimensions in that it carries out the secular goals of the state; because of this semi-public status conferred on the private school this institution has some claim to share in the public funds set aside by the state for the education of all of its future citizens.
2. Public welfare benefits surely include secular education, and by the rulings in *Cochran* and *Everson* the benefits extended by the state to all citizens may not be denied to anyone because of his religious faith or lack of it.

3. In the distribution of these public welfare benefits no Supreme Court opinion has held that the only constitutional formula is one which prevents even some incidental aid to religion. The Sunday-law decisions, in fact, expressly hold that the state is not precluded from implementing its secular goals in a way which bestows some collateral benefits on religion.

4. In view of clear Supreme Court rulings precluding sectarian teaching and religious practices in public schools it can be persuasively argued that the granting of funds only to the public school is a violation of the establishment clause because such a policy endorses and prefers one educational and philosophical orthodoxy over all others. This is the very essence of the Catholic case.

It seems fair to conclude that neither the Congress nor the Supreme Court of the United States has confronted the claim which is being made by parents who are dissenters from the orthodoxy which the public school represents. No quotation seems more appropriate to express their sentiments and to affirm the spirit with which the entire controversy over church-related schools should be discussed than the ringing words of Mr. Justice Jackson in the *Barnette* decision: "If there is any fixed star in our constitutional constellation, it is that no official, high or petty, can prescribe what shall be orthodox in politics, nationalism, religion, or other matters of opinion or force citizens to confess by word or act their faith therein."[21]

[21] *Id.* at 642.

MURRAY A. GORDON

The Unconstitutionality
of Public Aid to
Parochial Schools

On the question of the separation of state funds and church schools
there is a reversal of the customary alignment of forces on issues
of constitutionality. Claims of unconstitutionality are usually associated with a defensive posture assumed by those otherwise unable
to find community support. It is seldom necessary to prove the unconstitutionality of something we do not wish to do; we avoid an
undesirable course of action because it is undesirable, and its constitutionality is irrelevant. Some consensus that an action should be
taken is normally expected before it becomes necessary to consider
the constitutionality of ends or means.

The view that it is unconstitutional to use public monies to
support parochial schools—the discussion here being confined to
the propriety of such aid to church-operated elementary and secondary schools—is not, however, that of a discordant minority
relying upon some technical, albeit constitutional, proposition.
There is no unequivocal popular consensus for public financing
of church schools.[1] On the contrary, virtually every state has re-

MURRAY A. GORDON is a member of the Bar of the United States
Supreme Court and of the State of New York.

[1] "Every test of public opinion discloses that a substantial majority op-

tained long-standing prohibitions against the use of tax funds for the construction or maintenance of sectarian schools.[2] Congress has never directly appropriated money for such a purpose, and while supporters of federal aid to parochial schools have combined with those opposed to federal aid for other reasons to block federal aid to the public schools, it seems clear that at congressional and executive hearings and conferences the sense of the public and the authorities has consistently been that church schools shall not be publicly financed.[3] As will be seen, the most compelling reasons, stemming from our strongest and current feelings about the respective roles of government, religion, and the schools, support the case against public funds for parochial schools. That the First Amendment as well as the laws of every state mandates that which consensus and reason suggest is another of the frequent demonstrations of how the Constitution tends to confirm and to be confirmed by the experience and sentiment of our people.

The Impact upon the Public School System of Public Aid to Parochial Schools

Because the assertion of the unconstitutionality of public financial aid to private sectarian schools is an expression of public policy confirmed by the Constitution, I would start discussion on the subject by considering the sources of that policy. The first is the understood effect of such aid on the public school system. We have been and are responsibly warned that such aid threatens the survival of the secular common schools.

The highest court of the State of New York has reported the

---

pose federal aid to parochial schools." Pfeffer, *Federal Funds for Parochial Schools? No*, 37 Notre Dame Law. 309 (1962).

According to a February 10, 1963, poll by the American Institute of Public Opinion, public opposition to such aid seems to be waning. The number of interviewees who thought federal aid should be given only to public schools was 44% as compared with 57% two years earlier, and those who approved of federal aid to church and private schools had increased from 36% to 49%. Public Opinion News Service Press Release, Feb. 10, 1963.

[2] See *Catholic Schools and Public Money*, 50 Yale L.J. 917 (1941).

[3] See Pfeffer, Church, State, and Freedom 478–94 (1953).

determination of a state legislative committee with reference to the privilege of state aid for educational systems. The committee's 1853 report declared that the state

could not grant this privilege to one sect without opening the door for applications from every sect in the State, and "in view of their number, the conflicting and contradictory nature of their tenets, we should regard as suicidal the attempt to embrace them in the system of our common schools, or sustain them by its funds." The committee predicted that a policy of that kind would completely ruin the common school system and would open the door for a dangerous and vicious controversy among the different religious denominations as to who should get the largest share of school funds.[4]

For reasons very like the quoted views of more than a century before, the General Board of the National Council of the Churches of Christ in the United States of America adopted the following policy statement on February 22, 1961:

We therefore do not consider it just or lawful that public funds should be assigned to support the elementary or secondary schools of any Church. The assignment of such funds could easily lead additional religious or other groups to undertake full scale parochial or private education with reliance on public tax support. This further fragmentation of general education in the United States would destroy the public school system or at least weaken it so gravely that it could not possibly adequately meet the educational needs of all the children of our growing society.[5]

The supporting study by George R. La Noue of Yale points out by way of substantiation that

[P]rivate and parochial schools have been growing at a faster rate than public schools since World War II. If public funds were available, this trend would accelerate. The normal disputes in local school systems which are now settled through democratic compromise might often result in the setting up of independent schools by dissident groups. Not only churches, but some social, political, and economic

---

[4] Judd v. Board of Education, 278 N.Y. 200, 209, 15 N.E.2d 576, 581 (1938).

[5] Quoted in LA NOUE, PUBLIC FUNDS FOR PAROCHIAL SCHOOLS? 1–2 (Dep't of Religious Liberty of the Nat'l Council of the Churches of Christ in the U.S.A., Studies of Church and State 1963).

groups might begin to build school systems. The trend toward private schools by middle and upper class urban whites would grow, and school integration in the South would be doomed. If the public school compromise is broken, one does not have to conjure up visions about John Birch or Black Muslim schools to see the potential of divisiveness and the inevitable deterioration of educational standards.

It is a myth that only large groups can build and maintain private school systems. Both the Seventh-day Adventists, with 317,000 members, and the Christian Reformed Church, with 242,000 members, have extensive nation-wide school systems. Even the Pillar of Fire Church, with only 5,100 members nationally, operates an elementary school in Chicago. If there were no economic or psychological barriers, how many school systems would there be in New York City; Omaha, Nebraska; or Redlands, California?

. . . . [I]t is one thing for the state to subsidize religious schools in a country where there is only one church or two or five. In the United States we have almost three hundred denominations. Is the government to pick and choose among them or aid them all?

The situation might be worse in the United States if public funds were given to sectarian schools. In most urban areas and some other parts of the country a weakened but still functioning public school system would probably survive. But in small and middle-size cities in the South and Middlewest, the Protestant majority is so large, that, were they to abandon public schools in favor of their own parochial school system, the public school system would collapse. If that happened, Catholic and especially Jewish minorities might face the alternative of continuing a very inferior educational system that their members could provide or going to school in an alien religious environment.[6]

Reinhold Niebuhr has similarly indicated the impossibility of total public financing of parochial schools

without inviting the confusion of a proliferation of tax-supported religious schools for all the sects of Christendom. A religiously pluralistic community is bound to react to this threat to both the unity of the community and to the integrity of the common public school.[7]

[6] *Id.* at 36–38. (Footnotes omitted.) Leland Jamison of Princeton University put the matter even more pungently: "There are 250 cults and sects in this country. I am disturbed about the consequences if every one of these 250 started setting up schools in this way. What kind of educational chaos would there be if everybody sets up his own school system?" Jamison, Discussion on the School Question, in RELIGION AND FREEDOM 24 (McDonald rep. 1958).

[7] Niebuhr, *A Plea for Tolerance*, The Atlantic Monthly, Aug. 1962, p. 77.

The imminent hazards for the secular public school system when government funds are used to support a parallel sectarian school system are implicit in the observations on the supposed obsolescence of the secular school made by Rev. Robert F. Drinan in the Spring of 1961:

> The "secular" school was the creation of a new and growing nation in the last century. America's religious sociology has changed radically since that time so that the "secular" school is no longer consistent with the conscience of a significant portion of the nation's citizens.[8]

One need not be an apologist for the public school system or its many deficiencies to be firmly convinced of the indispensability of its preservation. The substitution of an endless diversity of sectarian private schools for the common public school as a principal means of elementary and secondary education will promote not pluralism but a dangerous divisiveness. Home, family, neighborhood, and church already insure the child's thorough grounding in the separateness of his culture and his religion. Hopefully the public school affords the child his main experiential introduction to the people and practices of the larger community. Mr. Justice Frankfurter spoke wisely and of his own knowledge when he characterized the public school as "at once the symbol of our democracy and the most pervasive means for promoting our common destiny"[9] and as "the training ground for habits of community."[10]

The child whose society is insulated by his schooling as well as his home may be strengthened in the doctrine of that home and school, but he is not thereby fully exposed to those competing values from among which he will be expected, in a democracy, to make his own, free, individual choices. It is, of course, open to parents to strictly confine and regulate the area of such choice for their children, and these parents are constitutionally protected in their right to accomplish this by sending their children to private

[8] Drinan, *Should the State Aid Private Schools?* 7 Catholic Law. 135, 143 (1961).

[9] McCollum v. Board of Education, 333 U.S. 203, 231 (1948)

[10] *Id.* at 227.

schools at their own expense. But it would be disastrous to implement the right of such parents by means of public financing which would subvert or even impair the efficacy of the public school system in its service as "the most powerful agency for promoting cohesion among a heterogeneous democratic people"[11]—a service performed by obliging children of differing and even conflicting cultures, religions, and values to live and learn together at an early and malleable age.

Church Schools, Tax Monies, and Politics

Another vexing corollary of public financing of church schools is the prospect of religious participation in the political business of deciding who gets how much of tax-raised monies. The balanced ticket and other manifestations of political sensitivity to religious pressures remind us that even in this country religion and politics are not strangers to each other. But we neither expect nor relish overt religious intervention in our political forums, except as matters directly impinging upon the doctrine or integrity of religion are raised. Yet churches will compete with synagogues, and both with public schools, and all with hospitals, police, fire, and other agencies of government for the division of limited public funds if the state finances church schools.

The bitterness engendered by the current opposition of the Catholic Church to federal aid to public schools unless such aid is supplied to parochial schools is a gauge of the likely consequence of religious intervention in the competition for tax monies. At best, such strife promises to be unseemly—at worst, it could change differences of faith from a test of ideas to a test of strength. Votes and secular influence, not the suasions of heart, mind, or spirit, are the main levers for gaining access to an adequate portion of the government budget. The face of religion and of government in this country would be radically altered, and not for the better, if religious groups assumed the lobbying and pressure functions customary for other contestants for tax monies. For it is demonstrably the case that the historical and constitutional withdrawal of reli-

[11] *Id.* at 216.

gion from overt participation in our local and national struggles for political power is directly responsible for the freedom, the growth, and the diversity which characterize religion in the United States.

STATE AND FEDERAL CONSTITUTIONS, AND PUBLIC AID TO PAROCHIAL SCHOOLS

Public financing of schools is, with us, primarily a local and state function. The rise of the free public school was, therefore, largely a concern of the states and the municipalities, and it was there that the issue of the relation of religion to the public schools was first raised and resolved.

Few verdicts of history are clearer than the purposeful determination of the states to bar the church from public schools and the church schools from public funds. It is indisputable that "in every one of the states without exception it is unlawful to grant tax-raised funds for the support of church or parochial schools."[12] This unanimous decision was not by default. It followed full and often inflamed debate, including the extraordinary instance of a religious political party in this country, the Catholic Party of the 1841 campaign in New York. Mr. Justice Frankfurter has reviewed the story as follows:

New York and Massachusetts provide famous chapters in the history that established dissociation of religious teaching from State-maintained schools. In New York, the rise of the common schools led, despite fierce sectarian opposition, to the barring of tax funds to church schools, and later to any school in which sectarian doctrine was taught. In Massachusetts, largely through the efforts of Horace Mann, all sectarian teachings were barred from the common school to save it from being rent by denominational conflict. The upshot of these controversies, often long and fierce, is fairly summarized by saying that long before the Fourteenth Amendment subjected the States to new limitations, the prohibition of furtherance by the State of religious instruction became the guiding principle, in law and feeling, of the American people.[13]

[12] Pfeffer, *supra* note 1, at 314.

[13] McCollum v. Board of Education, 333 U.S. 203, 214–15 (1948).

As the financing of elementary and secondary schooling is mainly a local phenomenon, questions of public aid to religious schools could not rise to the level of a federal constitutional problem before the First Amendment provisions dealing with religion were held in 1934 to apply to the states by operation of the due process clause of the Fourteenth Amendment.[14] And since the First Amendment antedated the experience of the states in their resolution of the church-state struggle in the schools by means of explicit prohibitions against any admixture of church and state in education, the First Amendment's language makes no specific reference to church schools in its provision that "Congress shall make no law respecting an establishment of religion, or prohibiting the free exercise thereof. . . ." Correctly understood, however, the First Amendment is just as conclusive as the laws of the states in its prohibition of any direct or avowed governmental financial aid to parochial schools.

The First Amendment, so far as it relates to matters of religion, consists of two aspects: it first proscribes laws "respecting an establishment of religion" (the establishment clause) ; it then guarantees the free exercise of religion (the freedom-of-religion clause). It is now settled that Jefferson and particularly Madison were the architects of the first of the Amendments, and that the establishment clause reflected and incorporated their earlier experience in Virginia in barring the use of tax-raised funds to support religious teaching.

The Virginia Assessment Bill of 1784, entitled "A Bill Establishing a Provision for Teachers of the Christian Religion," proposed to impose taxes to be used for the support of religion.[15] Each taxpayer could choose the church to receive his share of the tax; the taxpayer was, in fact, permitted "the option of giving his tax to education."[16] The final enactment of this bill was forestalled and defeated only by Madison's great Memorial and Remonstrance of

[14] Hamilton v. Regents, 293 U.S. 245 (1934). An earlier suggestion to the same effect appeared in Meyer v. Nebraska, 262 U.S. 390, 399 (1923).

[15] Quoted in full text in Everson v. Board of Education, 330 U.S. 1, 72 (1947) (Rutledge, J., dissenting).

[16] ECKENRODE, SEPARATION OF CHURCH AND STATE IN VIRGINIA 100 (1910).

1785, which declared the independence of the state from religion and religion from the state. In it Madison asked:

Who does not see that . . . . the same authority which can force a citizen to contribute three pence only of his property for the support of any one establishment, may force him to conform to any other establishment in all cases whatsoever?[17]

The 1786 enactment in Virginia of Jefferson's Bill for Establishing Religious Freedom answered:

Well aware that Almighty God hath created the mind free; . . . that to compel a man to furnish contributions of money for the propagation of opinions which he disbelieves, is sinful and tyrannical. . . .

Be it therefore enacted by the General Assembly. That no man shall be compelled to frequent or support any religious worship, place or ministry whatsoever, nor shall be enforced, restrained, molested, or burthened in his body or goods, nor shall otherwise suffer on account of his religious opinions or belief. . . .[18]

These intentions—to maintain state and religion separate and apart and therefore to foreclose the exaction of even "three pence" by taxation to support religious instruction—are the historical substance of the establishment clause.

THE SUPREME COURT AND THE ESTABLISHMENT CLAUSE

Not until 1947 did the Supreme Court of the United States have its first occasion to review the full meaning of the establishment clause in relation to governmental aid to church schools.[19] In *Everson v.*

[17] The Memorial and Remonstrance Against Religious Assessments is set out in full text in Everson v. Board of Education, 330 U.S. 1, 63 (1947) (Rutledge, J., dissenting). The quoted portion appears on pp. 65–66.

[18] Quoted in full text in BLAU, CORNERSTONES OF RELIGIOUS FREEDOM IN AMERICA 74–75 (1949).

[19] The effect of the establishment clause was not discussed or mentioned in an earlier decision that invalidated state legislation forbidding the operation of private sectarian schools, Pierce v. Society of Sisters, 268 U.S. 510 (1925), or in one sustaining the distribution in Louisiana of state-supplied textbooks to parochial as well as public school pupils. Cochran v. Louisiana State Board of Education, 281 U.S. 370 (1930). In 1899, the Court found no establishment-clause violation in the District of Columbia's payments to a "secular corporation," operated by the Catholic Church for the construction of a hospital and for supplying hospital care for indigent pa-

Board of Education,[20] the Court held that it was constitutional to reimburse the parents of parochial as well as public school pupils for the cost of transporting the children to school by public buses. (The case was decided 5 to 4, and one member of the majority, Mr. Justice Douglas, has since said that the decision "seems in retrospect to be out of line with the First Amendment."[21]) In writing for the Court Mr. Justice Black emphasized that any direct aid to the parochial schools would be violative of the First Amendment and that the incidental aid to sectarian schools resulting from transporting children to safeguard them from traffic hazards was no more proscribed than the incidental aids to religion occasioned by the police, fire, highway, and sewage disposal facilities which the state supplies church schools in common with all other members of the public.

The *Everson* Court, though sharply divided on the proper application of governing principles, manifested no dissent from Justice Black's formulation of those principles:

The "establishment of religion" clause of the First Amendment means at least this: Neither a state nor the Federal Government can set up a church. Neither can pass laws which aid one religion, aid all religions, or prefer one religion over another. Neither can force nor influence a person to go to or to remain away from church against his will or force him to profess a belief or disbelief in any religion. No person can be punished for entertaining or professing religious beliefs or disbeliefs, for church attendance or non-attendance. No tax in any amount, large or small, can be levied to support any religious activities or institutions, whatever they may be called, or whatever form they may adopt to teach or practice religion. Neither a state nor the Federal Government can, openly or secretly, partici-

---

tients of all religions. Bradfield v. Roberts, 175 U.S. 291 (1899). A few years later the Court saw no First Amendment objections to the use of Indian tribal trust funds to pay for parochial school training desired by members of the tribe. Quick Bear v. Leupp, 210 U.S. 50 (1908).

Neither *Cochran* nor *Quick Bear* explored or discussed the constitutional standards governing the interaction of government and church in the matter of the use of tax monies.

[20] 330 U.S. 1 (1947).

[21] Engel v. Vitale, 370 U.S. 421, 443 (1962).

pate in the affairs of any religious organizations or groups and *vice versa*. In the words of Jefferson, the clause against establishment of religion by law was intended to erect "a wall of separation between Church and State."[22]

. . . . New Jersey cannot consistently with the "establishment of religion" clause of the First Amendment contribute tax-raised funds to the support of an institution which teaches the tenets and faith of any church.[23]

If authoritative, the quoted *Everson* formulation settled the unavailability of direct public aid to parochial schools. Not unnaturally, the formulation was challenged by some proponents of such aid as obiter dictum, unrelated, unnecessary, and even contrary to the decision of the case. But while, as indicated, the result of the *Everson* case has been repudiated by the margin of the majority, and while six states have since interpreted their constitutions to prohibit the state to transport or to pay for the transportation of church school students,[24] the *Everson* formulation has been accorded remarkable recognition and approval by the Court. In three later majority opinions the entirety of that formulation has been quoted as the authoritative statement of the meaning of the establishment clause.[25] Plainly the *Everson* formulation (and its purpose to invalidate direct public financing of parochial schools) is the law of the First Amendment as read by the Supreme Court. The later cases leave no doubt on this score.

In *McCollum v. Board of Education*[26] the Court had before it the Champaign, Illinois, program in which public school classrooms were used for the conduct of religious instruction for thirty minutes

[22] 330 U.S. at 15–16.   [23] *Id*. at 16.

[24] Matthews v. Quinton, 362 P.2d 932 (Alaska 1961), *appeal dismissed and cert. denied*, 368 U.S. 517 (1962) ; Silver Lake Consol. School Dist. v. Parker, 238 Iowa 984, 29 N.W.2d 214 (1947) ; McVey v. Hawkins, 364 Mo. 44, 258 S.W.2d 927 (1953) ; Zellers v. Huff, 55 N.M. 501, 236 P.2d 949 (1951) ; Visser v. Nooksack Valley School Dist., 33 Wash.2d 699, 207 P.2d 198 (1949) ; Reynolds v. Nusbaum, 17 Wis.2d 148, 115 N.W.2d 761 (1962).

[25] Torcaso v. Watkins, 367 U.S. 488, 492–93 (1961) ; McGowan v. Maryland, 366 U.S. 420, 443 (1961) ; McCollum v. Board of Education, 333 U.S. 203, 210–11 (1948).

[26] 333 U.S. 203 (1948).

one day a week. Only those children whose parents requested such instruction participated in the program. The participating children were released from regular classes while receiving instruction. The Court found that the program was inconsistent with the establishment clause, which keeps religion and government each "free from the other within its respective sphere."[27] The dividing line between state and church was held to have been trespassed in two respects: (1) public property, in the form of school rooms, was used to promote religious teaching; and (2) the state's compulsory educational machinery was an integral part of the procedure whereby the religious instruction classes acquired attendants. Only one member of the Court, Mr. Justice Reed, dissented, and he agreed that "Of course, no tax can be levied to support organizations intended 'to teach or practice religion.' "[28]

In 1952, four years after *McCollum*, the Court upheld the New York released-time program which differed from that of Champaign mainly in that the religious instruction was conducted off the school premises.[29] The majority opinion, written by Mr. Justice Douglas, affirmed that separation of church and state "must be complete and unequivocal. . . . [T]he prohibition is absolute."[30] "Government," the Court said, "may not finance religious groups nor undertake religious instruction."[31] But, over the stinging dissents of Justices Black, Frankfurter, and Jackson, the Court found none of these doctrines impaired by the mere release of children to take religious training without the use of school property. The critical point of distinction made by the Court between this case and *Mc-collum*—the non-use of public property for a religious purpose—emphasizes the Court's consistent understanding that the state may not directly or avowedly give or lend its property, resources, or auspices to a religious project.

Last year, in deciding that the New York Regents' nondenominational public school prayer was in conflict with the establishment clause, the Court extended the doctrine of separation of church and

[27] *Id*. at 212.   [28] *Id*. at 249.

[29] Zorach v. Clauson, 343 U.S. 306 (1952).

[30] *Id*. at 312.   [31] *Id*. at 314.

state to its furthest reach to date. Without reference to previous decisional law as authority, and without reliance upon the use of public property for a religious end, the majority opinion in *Engel v. Vitale*[32] simply found that government has no place in the business of composing and sponsoring religious prayers to be recited by public school children. This finding was derived from the proposition that the establishment clause's "first and most immediate purpose rested on the belief that a union of government and religion tends to destroy government and to degrade religion."[33] Only Mr. Justice Stewart dissented. In a concurring opinion Mr. Justice Douglas took the occasion to say:

The point for decision is whether the Government can constitutionally finance a religious exercise. Our system at the federal and state levels is presently honeycombed with such financing. Nevertheless, I think it is an unconstitutional undertaking whatever form it takes.[34]

From the temper of the United States Supreme Court writings on the meaning of the establishment clause in defining the proper respective roles of church schools and the state, it must be concluded that the Court would, if confronted with the question, undoubtedly consider direct and avowed public financial aid to a parochial school as an impermissible breach of the wall separating church and state.

This construction of the First Amendment is shared by at least one branch of the federal government with the co-ordinate duty to comply with the Constitution. As a candidate for the Presidency, the then Senator Kennedy said, in April of 1960, as to federal assistance to parochial schools: "I am opposed to it. I believe it is clearly unconstitutional."[35] Later in the same campaign he declared that "I believe in an America where the separation of Church and State is absolute . . . . where no church or church school is granted any public funds or political preference. . . ."[36] Likewise, the 1961 Memorandum of the Department of Health, Education, and

[32] 370 U.S. 421 (1962).   [33] *Id.* at 431.   [34] *Id.* at 437.
[35] N.Y. Times, Apr. 22, 1960, p. 16, col. 2 (city ed.).
[36] N.Y. Times, Sept. 13, 1960, p. 22, col. 2 (city ed.).

Welfare on the constitutionality of federal aid to education, prepared at the request of Senator Wayne Morse, Chairman of the Education Subcommittee of the Senate Committee on Labor and Public Welfare, concluded, and for constitutional reasons, that "across-the-board grants to church schools may not be made"; that "across-the board loans to church schools are equally invalid"; and that "tuition payments for all church school pupils are invalid since they accomplish by indirection what grants do directly."[37] The memorandum acknowledged as constitutional some incidental aid to church schools resulting as a by-product of services provided by the state to all its citizens, but was nevertheless unequivocal in its judgment of the invalidity of direct aid: "The Supreme Court has made it absolutely clear that public funds and public property may not be used for the purpose of assisting any or all religions."[38]

It is, perhaps, suggestive of how firmly the United States Supreme Court has fixed the law on the subject of direct aid to church schools that the Legal Department of the National Catholic Welfare Conference, in the course of a most searching analysis of the Health, Education, and Welfare memorandum, expressly prefaced its analysis with the disclaimer that it would "not deal with the constitutionality of legislation which has financial benefit to church-related schools as its primary purpose or effect."[39] Of similar significance is the opinion expressed recently on the subject of church and state by a leading Catholic analyst, Dr. James M. O'Neill, at a seminar conducted by the Fund for the Republic: "Catholic education authorities have never asked for anything approaching full support on a parity with public education. It is my guess that if they were offered such support, it would be flatly refused."[40]

[37] Dep't of Health, Education, and Welfare, *Memorandum on the Impact of the First Amendment to the Constitution upon Federal Aid to Education,* Sen. Doc. No. 29, 87th Cong., 1st Sess. 5, 6 (1961), reprinted in 50 GEO. L.J. 349, 351–52 (1961).

[38] *Id.* at 15, 50 GEO. L.J. at 365.

[39] Legal Department, National Catholic Welfare Conference, *The Constitutionality of the Inclusion of Church-Related Schools in Federal Aid to Education,* 50 GEO. L.J. 397, 401–402 (1961).

[40] O'Neill, Discussion on the School Question, in RELIGION AND FREEDOM 21 (McDonald rep. 1958).

CONSIDERATION OF ARGUMENTS THAT TAX MONIES MAY
  BE CONSTITUTIONALLY APPROPRIATED TO THE
  USE OF CHURCH SCHOOLS

The proponents of the proposition that the Constitution allows direct public aid to parochial schools sponsor supporting arguments that have not found any substantial acceptance in the legal or judicial community. Thus the argument is made that church schools, which educate almost 15 per cent of all pupils attending elementary and secondary schools of the United States, are entitled to financial support from those governments whose education costs have been decreased by the education services supplied by sectarian schools. But the education services of church schools are not rendered at the instance of the state, nor is a saving to the state the purpose or objective of such instruction. Religious instruction is calculated to strengthen religious faith and convictions, and the state may not constitutionally support such a project, even if incidental savings to the state can be shown.

One of the distinguishing characteristics of twentieth-century government in the United States is its increasing involvement in social service functions. These functions frequently overlap with comparable services performed by private agencies throughout our society. The work of private organizations in hospitals, welfare agencies, and all manner of charities is frequently indistinguishable from that of the related government agencies. Consequently, many private social service agencies diminish, in some measure, costs and expenses which would otherwise be borne by government. This obviously does not entitle these agencies to state aid in each of these areas. Similarly the decrease in attendance at the public schools because of the church schools does not give the latter any constitutional right to state aid.

It has also been contended that the denial of state aid to church schools, when considered in conjunction with the compulsory-education laws and the secular nature of the public schools, is an infringement of the freedom of religion clause of the First Amendment.[41] This thesis runs as follows: The compulsory education laws

[41] See Drinan, *supra* note 8, *passim.*

oblige parents to send their children to elementary and secondary schools; the public schools are wholly secular in nature and therefore in conflict with the religious precepts of many parents; the Constitution permits parents to select the schools to which they will send their children, provided the schools maintain minimum educational standards; many parents are therefore obliged by their religious faiths and permitted by the Constitution to send their children to sectarian schools compatible with the religion of those parents; those parents who send their children to church schools for the indicated religious reasons pay taxes to maintain the common school and tuition for the parochial school and are thereby subjected to a severe financial burden to the detriment of the free exercise of their religion.

At bottom this contention means that in the instance of compulsory education, the requirement of the establishment clause that taxes may not be exacted to finance sectarian instruction is in conflict with the freedom of religion clause. It would, no doubt, have surprised Jefferson and others historically identified with the First Amendment and the concept of free public education to learn that the First Amendment was thus at war with itself or that there was any incompatibility between the First Amendment and our public school system. In fact, if the described contention is correct, then the whole history of free elementary and secondary education in this country, financed by tax funds and without comparable public aid to the church schools, has been at variance with the analogues of the First Amendment to be found in the constitutions of the several states.

If Quakers may constitutionally be taxed to support armies and weapons which violate their religious beliefs, taxpayers whose religious sensibilities are offended by religious neutrality in public school instruction may be constitutionally taxed to support secular public schools. And if, as the United States Supreme Court held in *Hamilton v. Regents*,[42] a Quaker can constitutionally be compelled to forego the financial advantage of attendance at a public university because of his unwillingness, for religious reasons, to take the

[42] 293 U.S. 245 (1934).

mandatory course in military training at that university, parents who elect, for religious reasons, to forego the financial advantage of a free public education for their children are likewise without sound constitutional complaint. That the religious freedom to send children to sectarian schools may be a financial burden does not amount to proof of unconstitutionality. The recent Supreme Court decisions sustaining various Sunday-closing laws over objections that such laws cause great financial loss and hardship to those obliged by religion to keep their places of business closed on another day of the week in addition to Sunday,[43] foreclose the proposition that the exercise of religion must be financially free in order to be constitutionally free. Of course, government may not impose financial or any other burdens upon religion *qua* religion. But where the exercise of a valid function of government, such as the operation of a secular public school, does not bar the religious option of attendance at a church school and only incidentally imposes the costs of the exercise of that option, there has been no denial of freedom of religion.

Nor does the compulsory-attendance feature of our educational systems support any claim of prejudice to the church schools. For it is not this feature which forces the alleged Hobson's choice between a free, but secular, public school and a costly, private, sectarian school. No realistic appraisal of contemporary society would suppose that many parents would deny their children elementary- and secondary-school training, even in the absence of any legal compulsion, so long as such schooling remained available tuition-free. Moreover, compulsory education must obviously enhance, rather than impair, church-school attendance. To the extent that compulsory school-attendance brings to the schools those who would otherwise enjoy the delights of guiltless truancy, the church schools as well as the public schools are the beneficiaries. It may, for purposes of advocacy, be expedient to structure constitutional issues on the base of the effect of compulsory education upon freedom of religion, but I doubt that the church schools would be will-

[43] Braunfeld v. Brown, 366 U.S. 599 (1961); Gallagher v. Crown Kosher Super Market, 366 U.S. 617 (1961).

ing to entertain the suggestion that compulsory-education laws be stricken because of their alleged unconstitutional consequences.

Finally, it has been argued that direct state aid is permissible so long as it is confined to that aspect of religious schooling which is only secular in nature.[44] Precisely how such an allocation would be made, particularly in respect to capital and administration or overhead costs, or who would distinguish the secular from the religious has not yet been itemized. The irremediable difficulty of the proposal is that in no course or facility is the religious aspect of a sectarian church school capable of being isolated. Even courses with no plain religious content, when taught in the religious surroundings of a church school, are a propagation of religious doctrine. That, in fact, is the ultimate reason for teaching all subjects, including the secular, in a church school. The child who is surrounded by religious symbols and taught by a religious figure (frequently in religious garb) is being subjected to and molded by religious influences, no matter the subject of the lesson. It has been said by the Court of Appeals of the State of New York that there "can be little doubt" that the effect of wearing of religious garb by a teacher, even in a public school classroom, would be to exert an "influence [which] was sectarian."[45] A due respect for the universality and the all-pervasiveness of any significant religion compels the conclusion that religiosity plays a role in the presentation of any subject of learning at a parochial school. Both the form and the substance of teaching in a church school effectively foreclose any public aid to so-called secular instruction by a church school.

[44] Legal Department, National Catholic Welfare Conference, *supra* note 39, at 420, 434–37.

[45] O'Connor v. Hendrick, 184 N.Y. 421, 428, 77 N.E. 612, 614 (1906) ; *cf.* Zellers v. Huff, 55 N.M. 501, 525, 236 P.2d 949, 964 (1951) : "Not only does the wearing of religious garb and insignia have a propagandizing effect for the church, but by its very nature it introduced sectarian religion into the [public] school"; West Virginia State Board of Education v. Barnette, 319 U.S. 624, 632 (1943) : "[T]he church speaks through the Cross, the Crucifix, the altar and shrine, and clerical raiment. . . . [R]eligious symbols come to convey theological [ideas]." See also 2 STOKES, CHURCH AND STATE IN THE UNITED STATES 292 (1950) ; Blum, *Religious Liberty and the Religious Garb,* 22 U. CHI. L. REV. 875 (1955) ; Note, 3 WAYNE L. REV. 57 (1956).

INDIRECT AID TO PAROCHIAL SCHOOLS—A TEST FOR VALIDITY

Direct public aid to denominational instruction being impermissible, the remaining question is whether so-called incidental or indirect aid to sectarian schools is within the limits allowed by the First Amendment.[46] As we have seen, the Supreme Court, by the narrowest margin, has sustained the incidental, indirect aid which accrued to church schools when parents of students of those schools were reimbursed for transportation costs. The Health, Education, and Welfare Department memorandum considered the public provision of free milk and hot lunches to parochial school children likewise to be a permissible indirect aid.[47]

The underlying rationale for incidental or indirect aid, developed in *Everson*, is that the state protects and serves all members of the community, including churches, church schools, and members of churches and church schools, in the performance of various services such as the maintenance of police, fire, safety, and health forces. The indirect aid to religion occasioned by these services is, of course, unavoidable. To exclude churches or church schools from those services because of their religious nature would be to discriminate against religion, probably a violation of the freedom of religion clause. It would, of course, be unthinkable to suggest that the establishment clause requires churches and church schools to go without benefit of public police or fire protection, even if religion is aided thereby. The issue presented, however, is the extent to which the doctrine of indirect aid may constitutionally be extended in the field of sectarian education. Even more precisely, the inquiry is to determine when the payment of public funds for services or benefits, in which the public has a legitimate interest, is allowable where such payment is incidentally an aid to religion—an issue

[46] Professor Kurland has suggested that the religion clauses of the First Amendment constitute a single limiting precept that government cannot utilize the factor of religion as a standard for conferring a benefit or imposing a burden. KURLAND, RELIGION AND THE LAW 18 (1962). The conceptual and practical defects of that thesis are fully delineated in Pfeffer, *Religion-Blind Government*, 15 STAN. L. REV. 389 (1963).

[47] Dep't of Health, Education, and Welfare, *supra* note 37, at 17, 50 GEO. L.J. at 369.

which arises when the state pays for transportation to a church school or for textbooks, lunches, medical care, and the like.

The ultimate test of the permissibility of indirect aid is whether it is the church (or church institution) or the state that performs or controls the performance of the services paid for by the state.[48] The payment of tax monies for services performed or controlled by a church or church school is an improper public aid to religion; the payment of public funds for services performed by a secular or public agency is not in contravention of the establishment clause, even if it produces an indirect aid to religion. As will be seen, this test provides an objective standard for screening out those indirect aids or services that lend themselves to the propagation of religious doctrine.

It is reasonable to assume that services performed or controlled by a religious institution could and would be used to further the religious objectives of that institution, whereas services performed or controlled by a public body would be secular in purpose and form. This analysis permits a line to be drawn dividing permissible and impermissible indirect aid: government funds may be disbursed to or by public agencies subject to public control, even where the expenditures are ultimately beneficial to parochial school students and incidentally or indirectly of aid to the church institutions they attend. But where public funds are used to pay for, or to reimburse for, services rendered by or subject to the control of the church school, the aid is impermissible. Similarly, where a church or church school is the nexus between the recipient of a benefit and the public financial source therefor, then the expenditure is also unconstitutional.

Thus, the transportation of school children by a *public* bus, the provision for fire or police protection by *public* uniformed forces, or the maintenance of the streets, highways, or sewerage systems by

[48] Where public funds are paid to a sectarian institution for the performance of services requested by the paying government (as distinct from religious instruction that parents have selected in preference to public school instruction), different problems may arise. The standard here projected to test the constitutionality of indirect aid to parochial schools therefore does not purport to cover matters such as research contracts or grants to denominational schools.

public departments and agencies are each public functions performed by public agencies which can and must be publicly supported even if religion is incidentally aided thereby. Different considerations would obtain, and different results would follow, if a
church school sought public funds to pay for its private police or
fire department.

In this view of the dividing line between valid and invalid indirect aid, publicly dispensed lunches, milk, or medical services to
parochial school students are permissible. Closer questions arise in
connection with the supplying of textbooks by the state to church
school pupils. Even where such textbooks are prepared or approved
by public authorities, the use of the texts in an educational context
which is privately, rather than publicly, managed and administered
directly serves a religious educational purpose.[49] Reimbursement
of tuition to the parents or pupils at church schools is a direct, and
not an incidental, aid to the religious schools, since such aid
amounts to a direct payment for religious instruction by a sectarian
institution. As indicated, the Health, Education, and Welfare memorandum has correctly considered the reimbursement of such tuition
to be an unconstitutional aid to parochial schools.[50] This judgment
is in accord with the most recent decision on that subject by the
Supreme Court of Vermont, a decision which the United States
Supreme Court declined to review.[51]

SOME CONCLUSIONS

As of today, the unconstitutionality of direct aid to parochial
schools is clear, despite the heavy fog of disputation and contention
which has surrounded the subject. I believe it is also reasonably
clear, in the case of indirect aid, that it is unconstitutional to dis-
pense public funds to pay for services performed or controlled by a

[49] Dickman v. School Dist., 366 P.2d 533 (Ore. 1961), *cert. denied,* 371
U.S. 823 (1962), fully reviews the cases on the subject of state payment for
textbooks for church school pupils and concludes that such an expenditure is
unconstitutional.

[50] See text accompanying note 37 *supra.*

[51] Swart v. South Burlington Town School Dist., 122 Vt. 177, 167 A.2d 514
(1961), *cert. denied,* 366 U.S. 925 (1961).

religious institution, at least where the performance of those services facilitates the propagation of religious doctrine.

But the problem begins, not ends, with an understanding of the limits set by the Constitution. The rise in costs of education is awesome and will compel the church schools—which are considered indispensable to the preservation and propagation of certain faiths—to seek supplementary financing beyond voluntary contributions or the payment of tuition by parents. Many parochial schools have already reached the limits of the cost-free teaching services obtained from the dedicated religious. For such schools the expansion of teaching facilities to meet the onslaught of the crop of war babies has required and will continue to require unprecedented financing. Those same pressures for financial help which are being experienced in the public school system throughout the country are no less urgent in the case of the church schools, and we are told authoritatively that "massive spending solely for public schools would in time result in a critical weakening of church-related schools, presaging the ultimate closing of many of them."[52]

Mr. Justice Jackson has said that "Catholic education is the rock on which the whole structure [of the Church] rests."[53] The onrushing educational dilemma, which urgently requires an accommodation within our constitutional system, is how to keep that rock from sinking or from causing the public school system to founder on it. An accurate rendition of what the Constitution dictates will, at least, avoid the waste of hopes and resources caused by solutions based upon tenuous constitutional exegeses and will compel the development of the kind and volume of voluntary support which, in the last analysis, is the only true measure of devotion to religious institutions.

[52] Legal Department, National Catholic Welfare Conference, *supra* note 39, at 438.

[53] Everson v. Board of Education, 330 U.S. 1, 24 (1947) (dissenting opinion).

PAUL G. KAUPER

The Constitutionality of
Tax Exemptions
for Religious Activities

Tax exemptions in favor of non-profit religious activities[1] are a common and historically sanctioned feature of American law. The exemption from property tax of property used for a house of worship or for religious purposes is universal in our states, whether pursuant to express constitutional grant or authorization or by reason of legislation without express authorization.[2] Most states extend the exemption to the land on which the church is located; and others to the value of the parsonage and adjacent parking lots.[3]

PAUL G. KAUPER is Professor of Law, University of Michigan.

[1] Statutes generally provide that property held or operated for profit does not qualify for the religious exemption. *E.g.*, DEL. CODE ANN. tit. 9, § 8103 (Supp. 1962); ILL. ANN. STAT. ch. 120, § 500.2 (Smith-Hurd Supp. 1962); N.Y. REAL PROP. TAX LAW § 420. The important problems of interpretation posed by these statutes are outside the scope of this paper.

Unless otherwise indicated, it will be assumed herein that the exemption for religious purposes does not prefer or discriminate against any particular religious denomination. See generally case cited note 41 *infra* and accompanying text.

[2] *E.g.*, N.Y. CONST. art. 16, § 1 (constitutional grant); ILL. CONST. art. IX, § 3 (constitutional authorization); WASH. REV. CODE § 84.36.020 (1962) (statutory exemption without constitutional provision).

[3] *E.g.*, CAL. CONST. art. XIII, § 1½ (land); COLO. REV. STAT. § 137–12–4 (Perm. Supp. 1960) (parsonage); ILL. ANN. STAT. ch. 120, § 500.16 (Smith-Hurd Supp. 1962) (parking lot).

Some states impose maximum limits on the amount of land and value of parsonages qualifying for exemption.[4] Some constitutions or statutes require that the exempt property be used exclusively for religious purposes.[5] The significant questions of interpretation raised by these state provisions are thoroughly discussed by Professor Arvo Van Alstyne in his excellent article in the Ohio State Law Journal.[6]

Federal income-tax law permits deductions for contributions for religious as well as educational and charitable purposes, and organizations serving these purposes are exempt from income taxation.[7] Likewise, the federal estate- and gift-tax laws permit deductions for gifts for religious, educational, and charitable purposes;[8] state inheritance-tax laws specify similar deductions.[9] Finally, exemptions are often recognized under federal and state privilege, or excise, taxes where religious activities or organizations are involved.[10]

This paper will be concerned chiefly with state property-tax exemptions. Since these furnish the largest body of useful materials, they usually assume the central place in any discussion of the tax problem. Before exploring the federal and state constitutional aspects of such exemptions, however, it is helpful to refer briefly to

[4] *E.g.*, N.J. STAT. ANN. § 54:4–3.6 (Supp. 1962) (5 acres); COLO. REV. STAT. § 137–12–4 (Perm. Supp. 1960) ($6,000).

[5] *E.g.*, CAL. CONST. art. XIII, § 1½; MASS. ANN. LAWS ch. 59, § 5 (Supp. 1962).

[6] Van Alstyne, *Tax Exemption of Church Property*, 20 OHIO ST. L. J. 461 (1959).

[7] INT. REV. CODE OF 1954, §§ 170, 501. Deductions are limited to 5% of gross income for corporate taxpayers and 20% of adjusted gross income for individuals, except that individuals may also deduct an additional 10% for contributions to churches, schools, and hospitals.

[8] INT. REV. CODE OF 1954, §§ 2106(a), 2522(a).

[9] *E.g.*, WIS. STAT. ANN. § 72.04(1) (West 1957).

[10] For a survey of religious exemptions from various state and federal taxes, see Note, *Constitutionality of Tax Benefits Accorded Religion*, 49 COLUM. L. REV. 968 (1949); Note, *Taxation of Religious Organizations— Benefits Granted by Federal and State Governments*, 5 VILL. L. REV. 255 (1959).

the underlying considerations of economic and social policy urged in support of and in opposition to the preferred treatment.

Court opinions supporting tax exemption frequently mention that the legislature relieves privately owned property and activities of a non-profit character from taxation because they serve public welfare purposes for which public funds would otherwise have to be spent.[11] This is a *quid pro quo* theory. Because services of a public-purpose type, including educational and charitable activities, are rendered by churches, the state grants tax exemptions in recognition of the value of these services and the tax savings that accrue because the state need not provide them.

A further argument in support of state tax exemptions for church property and property used for religious purposes is that they are given in consideration of, and in order to encourage, the public benefits resulting from religion's promotion of morality, good citizenship, law, and order.[12] The following statement from an opinion of the United States Court of Appeals for the District of Columbia is typical:

Congress in granting tax exemption under this statute, like most of the states, was giving expression to a broad legislative purpose to grant support to elements in the community regarded as good for the community.[13]

Moreover, many feel that exempting churches from taxation relieves them of all governmental burdens, thus achieving the full and complete separation of church and state and implementing the church's total freedom of worship.

On the other hand, numerous arguments against the economic

[11] *E.g.*, Asylum v. New Orleans, 105 U.S. 362, 368 (1881); Fellowship of Humanity v. County of Alameda, 153 Cal. App. 2d 673, 696, 315 P.2d 394, 409 (1957); Milward v. Paschen, 16 Ill.2d 302, 309, 157 N.E.2d 1, 5 (1959).

[12] See Bell's Gap R.R. v. Pennsylvania, 134 U.S. 232, 237 (1890); First Unitarian Church v. County of Los Angeles, 48 Cal.2d 419, 438, 311 P.2d 508, 520 (1957), *rev'd*, 357 U.S. 545 (1958). See generally articles cited note 10 *supra*; Note, *Exemption of Educational, Philanthropic and Religious Institutions from State Real Property Taxes*, 64 Harv. L. Rev. 288 (1950).

[13] Washington Ethical Soc. v. District of Columbia, 249 F.2d 127, 129 (D.C. Cir. 1957).

and social wisdom of tax exemptions could be addressed to both the legislature and the various church groups. Certainly the churches receive the ordinary benefits of government, such as police and fire protection, for which they, like other citizens and organizations, ought to share the burden. Moreover, the amount of aid granted by tax exemption bears no logical relationship to the moral good or community welfare which any individual church might promote, but rather it is determined by the arbitrary and often accidental factor of property valuation. Even church members must recognize that non-members bear a heavier burden because of the exemptions; indeed, even the members of denominations with small property-holdings bear the burden of exemptions for wealthier churches with large holdings. The question may also be raised whether the churches, in the interest of fully preserving their status as free and independent institutions, should not prefer to shed the cloak of governmental favoritism and stand before the community on the strength of their own messages and missions, unfettered by state restrictions and unembarrassed by state aid.

Issues Raised under State Constitutions

Despite the universality and long history of exemptions of property used for worship or other religious purposes, questions respecting the constitutionality of these exemptions have only infrequently been raised before the state courts or discussed at length in state judicial opinions. This is largely because many state constitutions expressly create or authorize such exemptions. In the few instances where the problems raised under state constitutions have been dealt with by the courts, they have not been seen to present serious questions.

Constitutional provisions in many of the states either expressly create an exemption for property-tax purposes of property used for worship or other religious purposes or authorize the legislature to provide for such an exemption.[14] Such exemptions obviously raise no issue under the state constitution. But where a state legislature exercises its taxing power to create such an exemption, which is not

[14] See constitutions and statutes cited note 2 *supra*.

expressly recognized or authorized in the constitution, the validity of the exemption may be challenged on the ground that it violates a uniformity or equal-protection clause of the state constitution or that it is prohibited by a clause forbidding the use of public funds to aid religious activities, support or maintain a house of worship, or pay the salary of a teacher of religion.

When property-tax exemptions have been attacked as violations of the uniformity or equal-protection clauses of the state constitutions, the usual answer has been that these clauses do not preclude a legislative power to classify for tax purposes by creating exemptions resting on rational grounds. The rationality of tax exemptions is determined by a consideration of germane public interests that warrant relieving certain classes of persons from obligations otherwise imposed on all other persons. State courts have experienced no difficulty in finding that exemptions of property used for church or religious purposes are reasonable.[15]

A second objection is that the statutory grant of exemption of property used for a house of worship or for religious purposes violates state constitutional provisions which prohibit laws respecting an establishment of religion[16] or, more specifically, the use of tax funds to maintain houses of worship or a minister of religion.[17] The argument here is that by relieving churches of taxes imposed on property owners generally, the state is conferring a benefit which is equivalent to an appropriation of public funds in support of religious purposes. Or, to put the argument another way, the state—by furnishing the usual public services, such as police and fire protection, without securing a compensating payment in the form of

[15] See Mayor of Baltimore v. Minister and Trustees of Starr Methodist Protestant Church, 106 Md. 281, 285–87, 67 Atl. 261, 263 (1907) ; cases collected in Annot., 2 A.L.R. 471 (1919).

[16] E.g., UTAH CONST. art. I, § 4.

[17] E.g., MICH. CONST. art. II, § 3. See generally Paulsen, *State Constitutions, State Courts and First Amendment Freedoms*, 4 VAND. L. REV. 620, 635 (1951).

taxes—is making a gratuitous contribution in aid of a house of worship or minister of religion. The Iowa Supreme Court, in the only state-court decision in which this issue was directly contested, rejected this contention. Its argument was that, unlike a direct appropriation of public funds, a tax exemption is only indirect aid and not the kind forbidden by the constitution.[18] The Illinois Supreme Court, dealing with a related question, rejected the contention that an exemption for an educational institution operated by a religious denomination violated the state constitutional provision prohibiting legislative preference of any religious denomination or support of any ministry or place of worship. After noting that the tax exemption was non-discriminatory, the court said:

> ... [I]n a Christian nation such as ours it is important to the public good that there should be schools not devoted entirely to training or stimulating the brain or intellect, but that such teaching may also be supplemented by training and building the moral character and better impulses of the heart.[19]

The state-court decisions, then, point to the conclusion that tax exemptions violate neither the equal-protection or uniformity provision nor provisions prohibiting use of state tax funds for religious purposes. In reaching these conclusions the state courts have found that benefits to the public rendered by churches and their activities warrant the tax exemption. They have found, further, that any benefit to churches and religious activities is incidental or indirect and, as such, does not conflict with express state constitutional prohibitions against spending for sectarian purposes. These decisions and the provisions of state constitutions expressly authorizing such exemptions warrant the conclusion that, so far as the constitutional practice and interpretation of the states are concerned, a line is drawn between prohibited direct expenditures of public funds for religious purposes and permissible indirect aid by way of tax exemptions for churches and religious purposes.

[18] Trustees of Griswold College v. State, 46 Iowa 275 (1877).

[19] Garrett Biblical Institute v. Elmhurst Bank, 331 Ill. 308, 318, 163 N.E. 1, 4 (1928).

21748

ISSUES RAISED UNDER THE FEDERAL CONSTITUTION

The validity of any tax exemption benefiting churches or religious activities under the income- or estate- and gift-tax laws may be challenged under either the due process clause of the Fifth Amendment—in so far as it serves as a bar to arbitrary legislative classification—or, more specifically, under the First Amendment's language prohibiting laws respecting an establishment of religion.

In so far as federal constitutional limitations on the states' power to grant tax exemptions for property or transactions involving religious purposes is concerned, the two relevant limitations are the due process and equal protection clauses of the Fourteenth Amendment and the free-exercise and non-establishment clauses of the First Amendment. For purposes of our discussion we should assume, in the light of what the Supreme Court has said, that the First Amendment applies to the states.[20] However, I must confess that recent Supreme Court opinions affirming this idea[21] leave unclear in my mind whether the Fourteenth Amendment makes the First Amendment applicable per se without regard to any of the language used in the Fourteenth Amendment or whether the First Amendment's limitations are translated into limitations on the states through the language of Section 1 of the Fourteenth Amendment (more particularly, the due process and equal protection clauses). It may be said that a taxpayer is deprived of his property without due process of law if a church is granted a tax exemption that is found to violate the non-establishment limitation. More persuasively, it may be argued that the religion clauses of the First Amendment operate as a special rule of classification which should be written into the Fourteenth Amendment so that any state tax law which uses religion as a basis for classification, in order either to aid or hinder religion, raises a special issue under the equal protection limitation, as opposed to the usual question of reasonableness in classification. Whatever the theory, it is enough for our purposes to recognize that, according to the Supreme Court's opinions, the First Amend-

[20] *E.g.*, Murdock v. Pennsylvania, 319 U.S. 105, 108 (1943); Everson v. Board of Education, 330 U.S. 1 (1947).

[21] *E.g.*, Engel v. Vitale, 370 U.S. 421 (1962).

ment's religion clauses are applicable to the states, so that the validity of tax exemptions under state law may be examined by reference to both the free-exercise and the non-establishment limitations.

On the equal protection and due process questions raised under the federal constitution there is, again, a paucity of authority. For example, when the Supreme Court was called upon to interpret an act of Congress exempting churches in the District of Columbia from taxation, its opinion simply assumed the constitutionality of the exemption, noting that "Congress, like any State legislature unrestricted by constitutional provisions, may at its discretion wholly exempt certain classes of property from taxation."[22] However, in subsequent decisions dealing with the problem of tax classification generally the Court has made broad statements which suggest that it would agree with state decisions that tax exemptions for churches and religious purposes fall within the permissive area of legislative classification.[23]

It seems clear that the most substantial limitations relevant to tax exemptions, so far as the federal constitution is concerned, are imposed by the religion clauses of the First Amendment, which state that Congress shall make no law respecting an establishment of religion or prohibiting the free exercise thereof and which, by judicial interpretation, limit the states also.

The free-exercise clause is relevant in so far as it suggests that neither Congress nor the states can do anything that hinders or interferes with religious activities. But does the First Amendment require that churches and persons engaged in religious activities be exempt from federal or state taxes? The state courts have never seriously advanced the proposition that such exemptions are essential to religious freedom.[24] If we follow Professor Kurland's

[22] Gibbons v. District of Columbia, 116 U.S. 404, 408 (1885).

[23] See American Sugar Refining Co. v. Louisiana, 179 U.S. 89, 92 (1900); Bell's Gap R.R. v. Pennsylvania, 134 U.S. 232, 237 (1890).

[24] Indeed, it has been held that they clearly are not essential to religious freedom. Watchtower Bible and Tract Soc. v. Los Angeles County, 30 Cal.2d 426, 182 P.2d 178 (1947); *cf.* State v. Alabama Educational Foundation, 231 Ala. 11, 163 So. 527 (1935). See also note 29 *infra*.

thesis[25] that the First Amendment states a special rule prohibiting classification on the basis of religious activity as a means of either hindering or benefiting religion, then certainly no constitutional objection can be raised to the application to churches and religious activities of a general tax, such as a property tax, which does not by its terms or in its application discriminate on the ground of religion.

Nevertheless, in some decisions dealing with Jehovah's Witnesses, the United States Supreme Court has held that non-discriminatory excise taxes levied by municipalities were invalid in their application to religious activities—for instance, taxes on the sale of books and literature.[26] These decisions appear to rest on the premise that religious activities cannot be subject to privilege taxes, and they reflect the frequently expressed view that religious freedom is a constitutionally preferred freedom.[27] However, the Jehovah's Witnesses cases have, at most, a limited reach and extend to only one phase of the tax-exemption question. It must be remembered that they dealt with taxes that were levied directly on a privilege of engaging in activities which, in the cases before the Court, were identifiable as personal religious activities. These cases are not relevant to the issue whether property owned by churches or used in religious activities is entitled to a property-tax exemption in the name of religious liberty. Moreover, as the cases involving state taxation of interstate commerce amply demonstrate, a distinction is made between excises on activities privileged under the constitution and a tax on property used in such activities.[28] It is fair to suppose that just as interstate commerce can be made to pay its way by

25 See KURLAND, RELIGION AND THE LAW (1962).

26 Follett v. McCormick, 321 U.S. 573 (1944); Murdock v. Pennsylvania, 319 U.S. 105 (1943). Cf. Martin v. Struthers, 319 U.S. 141 (1943).

27 See, e.g., Thomas v. Collins, 323 U.S. 516 (1944); Prince v. Massachusetts, 321 U.S. 158, 173 (1944) (dissenting opinion).

28 See the discussion in McGoldrick v. Berwind-White Co., 309 U.S. 33, 45–47 (1940). There is a similar analogy in the case of state taxation of newspaper plants and publishing houses, which is permissible even though the freedom of the press guarantee prohibits an excise tax on the activity of publishing. Grosjean v. American Press Co., 297 U.S. 233 (1936).

being subjected to property and other types of non-discriminatory taxes, so can churches constitutionally be made to pay their way by being subject to non-discriminatory property taxes that compensate the state and local governments for services which the churches as well as other property owners enjoy. In other words, I feel that the Jehovah's Witnesses cases have a limited application and that in general the First Amendment's free-exercise clause does not require the usual exemptions accorded by state constitutional provisions or by statute for property held for church and other religious purposes.[29]

A more difficult question is whether the First Amendment's non-establishment clause forbids either Congress or the states from granting preferential tax exemptions on the basis of religious activity. Does the granting of such exemptions by statute amount to a law respecting an establishment of religion? In 1947, in the famous *Everson* case,[30] the Supreme Court for the first time used the non-establishment clause as a basis for determining whether the action of a state agency in disbursing public funds was invalid because it was claimed to confer a benefit on a religious activity, namely, the operation of parochial schools. In the course of his much publicized opinion in this case, Justice Black said that the First Amendment's religion clauses established the constitutional principle of separation of church and state; that they, indeed (to use Jefferson's phrase), ordained a wall of separation between church and state; that the non-establishment clause, among other things, prohibited a state from giving aid to any and all religions; and that no tax could be levied, whether large or small, to support religious activities or institutions.[31]

---

[29] See Braunfeld v. Brown, 366 U.S. 599, 606 (1961), where the Chief Justice quite clearly indicates, in an opinion for four members of the Court, that he would not regard as unconstitutional an income-tax statute which limits the amount which may be deducted for religious contributions, even though it imposes an indirect economic burden on the observance of the religion of the citizen whose religion requires him to donate a greater amount to his church. See also note 24 *supra*.

[30] Everson v. Board of Education, 330 U.S. 1 (1947).

[31] *Id*. at 15–16,

Thus there emerged from the *Everson* opinion the idea that the First Amendment does more than prohibit giving preferential aid or treatment to one or more churches. It prohibits the use of tax funds to aid any and all religious activities. Taken literally, this means that the federal government and the states must, as a constitutional matter, deny benefits to churches under general laws which do not single out religious activities for preferred treatment. I mention this since Professor Kurland, by treating the religion clauses of the First Amendment as a special classification principle, prohibiting laws which hinder or benefit religion as such, would have no difficulty in sustaining laws which aid religion and religious activities, so long as this aid is not preferential and results from a broader classification that includes religious activities but is not confined to them. But as I understand the no-aid idea advanced by the Supreme Court as an abstract theory or proposition, it rises above a classification principle and prohibits government, out of deference to the separation idea, from any practice or law which is found to aid religious activities, whether on a preferential basis or not.

Starting then with the proposition that the non-establishment clause prohibits governmental aid to religion, tax exemptions for churches raise the critical question whether this is the kind of aid forbidden by the First Amendment. No one can doubt that churches derive an economic benefit from the tax exemptions accorded their property.[32] If a state were to make outright grants to churches out of tax funds in amounts equal to the taxes that would be levied but for exemptions, this would clearly violate the First Amendment as construed in *Everson*.

Notwithstanding the relevancy of the non-establishment limitation, construed as a no-aid-to-religion principle, no court, to my knowledge, has yet declared a tax exemption invalid under the First

[32] See generally Paulsen, *Preferment of Religious Institutions in Tax and Labor Legislation*, 14 LAW & CONTEMP. PROB. 144 (1949) ; Stimson, *The Exemption of Property from Taxation in the United States*, 18 MINN. L. REV. 411 (1934) ; Note, *Taxation of Religious Organizations—Benefits Granted by Federal and State Governments*, 5 VILL. L. REV. 255 (1960) ; Comment, *State Tax Exemptions and the Establishment Clause*, 9 STAN. L. REV. 366 (1957).

Amendment.[33] The question as raised under the First Amendment
has been slow in coming before the courts. This is not surprising,
since the applicability of the First Amendment, interpreted in terms
of the no-aid idea as a limitation on the states, was not determined
until 1947 when the *Everson* case was decided. Since then the tax-
exemption issue has not been directly presented to the Supreme
Court for consideration. The Court has passed upon school released-
time plans for religious instruction of children,[34] upon Sunday-closing laws,[35] and recently upon a prayer prescribed for use in public
schools.[36] But all these cases, while dealing with the non-establishment clause, were concerned with the affirmative use of state police
and tax powers to aid religion or promote religious practices. They
are, therefore, not directly applicable to tax exemptions which involve indirect aid. However, Justice Douglas' far-ranging concurring opinion in the Regents'-prayer case does suggest that, in his
opinion, any financial assistance accorded by government to religion would be invalid.[37] In none of the various opinions in these
cases are tax exemptions expressly mentioned except in Justice
Reed's dissenting opinion in the *McCollum* released-time case,
where he pointed to freedom from taxes as one of the incidental ad-
vantages which religious and other similar bodies obtain as a by-
product of organized society.[38]

The relevancy of the First Amendment to property-tax exemptions has been questioned in a few recent state-court decisions,

[33] However, it was suggested in Watchtower Bible and Tract Soc. v. Los
Angeles County, 181 F.2d 739, 741 (9th Cir. 1950), that to isolate a religious
corporation because of its religious character and *require* the state and municipalities to grant property-tax exemptions to it might violate the non-establishment requirement.

[34] McCollum v. Board of Education, 333 U.S. 203 (1948); Zorach v. Clauson, 343 U.S. 306 (1952).

[35] McGowan v. Maryland, 366 U.S. 420 (1961); Two Guys from Harrison-
Allentown, Inc. v. McGinley, 366 U.S. 582 (1961); Gallagher v. Crown Kosher
Super Market, Inc., 366 U.S. 617 (1961); Braunfeld v. Brown, 366 U.S. 599
(1961).

[36] Engel v. Vitale, 370 U.S. 421 (1962).

[37] *Id.* at 437–44.

[38] McCollum v. Board of Education, 333 U.S. 203, 249 (1948).

which are of special interest here. In *Lundberg v. County of Alameda*[39] the California Supreme Court considered the validity of a statute which exempted property of educational institutions, including parochial schools, from taxation. The court, after finding that the exemption was warranted under the provision of the state constitution expressly exempting property owned and used for charitable purposes, rejected the argument that an exemption for parochial schools violated the First Amendment. More recently, the Rhode Island Supreme Court in *General Finance Corp. v. Archetto*[40] has upheld a property-tax exemption for churches in the face of the First Amendment argument. Mention should also be made of the California District Court of Appeals' decision in *Fellowship of Humanity v. County of Alameda*[41] which, while sustaining the constitutionality of a property-tax exemption for churches as not constituting an unlawful establishment of religion, went on to hold that such an exemption would be unconstitutional as discriminatory unless it were extended to property used for regular assembly by a non-theistic religious organization.

The opinions in these cases offered no clear-cut or compelling reasoning on the First Amendment question. The California Supreme Court found that the holding and reasoning of the *Everson* case could be used to support a tax exemption of property used for parochial school purposes. Tax exemptions for religious activities generally were said to be sanctioned by their universality. The California Court also referred approvingly to the Supreme Court's statement in *Zorach*, that these were questions of degree and it concluded that the First Amendment was not intended to invalidate tax exemptions.[42]

In meeting the arguments derived from *Everson* and *McCollum* that tax exemptions in aid of religious purposes were a forbidden form of establishment the Rhode Island Supreme Court stated its

---

[39] 46 Cal.2d 644, 298 P.2d 1 (1956), *appeal dismissed sub nom.* Heisey v. County of Alameda, 352 U.S. 921 (1956).

[40] 176 A.2d 73 (R.I. 1961), *appeal dismissed*, 369 U.S. 423 (1962).

[41] 153 Cal. App. 2d 673, 315 P.2d 394 (1957).

[42] Lundberg v. County of Alameda, *supra* note 39, at 654–55, 298 P.2d at 7–8.

opinion that such exemptions do not constitute direct participation by state authorities in the promotion of religious education, pointed to the *Zorach* opinion as limiting the sweeping language of *Everson*, noted that it is not possible to get from the various opinions of the Supreme Court any valid generalization on the meaning of the First Amendment, and concluded that the Supreme Court had not gone so far as to hold that tax exemptions are clearly and beyond a reasonable doubt invalid under the First Amendment.[43] In closing its opinion the Rhode Island court quoted Justice Reed's dissenting statement in *McCollum*, that "devotion to the great principle of religious liberty should not lead us into a rigid interpretation of the constitutional guarantee that conflicts with accepted habits of our people."[44] The California appellate court in the *Fellowship of Humanity* case justified tax exemptions for a house of worship on the ground that the church was used for some purposes—educational and social—which were not strictly religious and that these purposes promote public interest in morality and law and order.[45]

In short, the recent state-court decisions dealing with possible First Amendment limitations on state tax exemptions have reached results consistent with earlier decisions arising under state constitution and have relied on much the same arguments—the exemptions of property used for houses of worship and other religious purposes are universal and well rooted in history; they are not a direct aid to religious activities; and they find their justification in the social benefits resulting from churches and religious activities.

What may seem surprising is that the United States Supreme Court dismissed the appeals taken from the decisions of the California and Rhode Island Supreme Courts on the ground that they did not raise substantial federal questions.[46] Justices Black and Frankfurter dissented from dismissal of the appeal in *Lundberg*

[43] General Finance Corp. v. Archetto, *supra* note 40, at 77–78.

[44] *Id.* at 78–79.

[45] Fellowship of Humanity v. County of Alameda, *supra* note 41, at 693–98, 315 P.2d at 405–08.

[46] Heisey v. County of Alameda, 352 U.S. 921 (1956); General Finance Corp. v. Archetto, 369 U.S. 423 (1962).

and Justice Black dissented in *Archetto,* with Justices Frankfurter and White not taking part. The Court could have chosen either of these cases to declare its views on tax exemptions as affected by the First Amendment's religion clauses. It not only chose not to do so, but in saying by a very clear majority that no substantial federal issue was raised, it arguably held that tax exemptions for houses of worship and for parochial schools raise no real issue with respect to the establishment of religion. But whatever weight may be given to the Court's action as a matter of logic, it is clear as a practical matter that it would be hazardous and premature to say that the dismissal of these appeals has given a definitive or final answer to the problem. There are enough instances of the Court itself failing to consider such dispositions binding, so that one should be very cautious about deeming them conclusive on the substantive issues.[47] It is therefore worthwhile to consider the factors that may be relevant in the determination of this issue.

On its face a tax exemption of property used for worship or other religious purposes does constitute a substantial economic aid to religion, and its constitutionality is, therefore, subject to doubt. The fact that it is extended indiscriminately to all types of religion should make no difference according to the prevailing interpretation of the First Amendment language. Likewise, if the no-aid principle is an independent limitation, it should make no difference that the exemption for churches is part of an over-all exemption for property of all non-profit organizations serving charitable purposes in the broad and historic sense of this term. Moreover, to determine whether the exemption applies in a given case requires the courts to undertake the difficult task of determining and defining what is meant by a house of worship or by religious activities and purposes. Also, the obtaining of tax exemptions puts churches in the position of being debtors to the state and may suggest to some an

---

[47] For example, prior to its decision in the Sunday-closing cases in 1961, the Supreme Court had on several occasions dismissed appeals for want of a substantial federal question in cases involving similar types of statutes. Kidd v. Ohio, 358 U.S. 132 (1958); Towery v. North Carolina, 347 U.S. 925 (1954); McGee v. North Carolina, 346 U.S. 802 (1953); Friedman v. New York, 341 U.S. 907 (1951).

impairment of the free and voluntary character attributed to churches in our system. It is asserted, moreover, that these exemptions have their roots in a time when the states had their established religions[48]—a far cry from the present situation. All these considerations suggest that tax exemptions should now be found to violate the separation principle distilled from the First Amendment.

The first argument in support of the constitutionality of tax exemptions is the very solid consideration that tax exemptions for churches are universal in this country and have a long history. This history cannot be explained solely as a carry-over from the earlier days of established churches. These exemptions are found also in states formed and organized after churches had been disestablished in the colonial states. In many states they have also been recently amended to extend the scope of the exemption. This suggests a rationally conceived and deep-seated policy, and not an accidental or vestigial survival of outmoded practices. The impressive historical argument assumes even greater significance when the attempt is made to use the First Amendment's ambiguous language to outlaw tax exemptions for churches on the theory that the Fourteenth Amendment, adopted in 1868, made the First Amendment applicable to the states. Whether or not the latter theory rests on more than myth or spurious historical interpretation,[49] it is pertinent to note Justice Holmes's observation that the Fourteenth Amendment was not intended to undo two hundred years of history.[50] I recognize that the historical argument is not conclusive, as evidenced by the school-segregation[51] and school-prayer cases,[52] but its relevancy can hardly be challenged.

The Supreme Court's interpretations of the First Amendment by no means establish the invalidity of tax exemptions for churches.

[48] See generally, TORPEY, JUDICIAL DOCTRINES OF RELIGIOUS RIGHTS IN AMERICA, ch. 1 (1948).

[49] See Freund, *The Supreme Court and Civil Liberties*, 4 VAND. L. REV. 531 (1951); Fairman, *Does the Fourteenth Amendment Incorporate the Bill of Rights? The Original Understanding*, 2 STAN. L. REV. 5 (1949).

[50] Jackman v. Rosenbaum Co., 260 U.S. 22, 31 (1922).

[51] Brown v. Board of Education, 349 U.S. 294 (1955).

[52] Engel v. Vitale, 370 U.S. 421 (1962).

The notion that the non-establishment clause forbids all aid to religion cannot be literally applied—as indicated by the results in the *Everson* and *Zorach* cases, where the Court did in fact uphold expenditures of public money and uses of the public school program to aid religious activities.[53] In the *Zorach* opinion Justice Douglas stated that a legislature could accommodate the public school program to the religious needs of the people, since we are a religious people whose institutions presuppose a Supreme Being. Whether the recent New York prayer case means a repudiation of *Everson* and *Zorach* remains to be seen, but at least up to this point the Court has not defined "aid to religion" clearly enough to warrant the categorical conclusion that tax exemptions for churches are unconstitutional. In short, we cannot take at face value the absolute and sweeping language of some of the interpretations of the non-establishment limitation. We are dealing with questions of degree, as Justice Douglas pointed out in *Zorach*.[54]

Furthermore, the Supreme Court apparently treats the free-exercise and non-establishment clauses as independent limitations, and not as an integrated and unitary rule of classification that might prevent tax exemptions for religious organizations. In some instances the Court's problem is that of balancing the non-establishment or no-aid principle against the free-exercise principle. If, as Professor Katz suggests, the promotion of religious freedom and the observance of state neutrality in furtherance of this freedom is the over-all objective of the First Amendment, then it may be that in some situations the free-exercise principle may have to prevail over the no-aid principle.[55] This balancing idea, which of course runs counter to Professor Kurland's thesis, is accepted in some judicial opinions. The decisions upholding the right of Jehovah's Witnesses to the use of public parks for religious services[56] and the exemption of Jehovah's Witnesses from certain local excise

[53] See KAUPER, CIVIL LIBERTIES AND THE CONSTITUTION 11–19 (1962).

[54] Zorach v. Clauson, 343 U.S. 306, 314 (1952).

[55] Katz, *Freedom of Religion and State Neutrality*, 20 U. CHI. L. REV. 426 (1953). See also KAUPER, *op. cit. supra* note 53, at 35–37.

[56] Niemotko v. Maryland, 340 U.S. 268 (1951).

taxes[57] may be cited in this connection. Moreover, the Supreme Court's decisions indicate that in recognition of religious liberty and the religious interests of the people, the legislature may, at its discretion, grant exemptions from laws of general operation even though such exemptions are not constitutionally required and may, indeed, be questioned under the non-establishment clause. Congress may exempt from military service those who object on religious grounds,[58] a state may exempt children from the usual public school obligations in order to permit them to attend religious-education classes;[59] and a state may exempt from the limitations imposed by Sunday-closing laws those who on religious grounds observe a different day of rest.[60]

CONCLUSION

A determination of the constitutionality of tax exemptions for religious purposes is facilitated by distinctions between the various kinds of activity that may be benefited by the exemption. Churches and religious organizations engage in some enterprises that parallel those supported directly by government, such as education, hospitalization, and the relief of the poor. These in a broad sense may be called welfare enterprises. Since government itself supports programs of this kind and since they are recognized to serve public needs even when carried on by private agencies, tax exemptions for the private agencies seem appropriate on the ground, often stated by state courts, that the performance of these functions by private agencies saves the state the expense of providing these services.[61] Indeed, educational and welfare enterprises con-

[57] Cases cited note 26 *supra.*

[58] Selective Draft Law Cases, 245 U.S. 366, 389–90 (1917).

[59] Zorach v. Clauson, 343 U.S. 306 (1952).

[60] Commonwealth v. Arlan's Dept. Store, 357 S.W.2d 708 (Ky. 1961), *appeal dismissed for want of a substantial federal question,* 371 U.S. 218 (1962); Braunfeld v. Brown, 366 U.S. 599, 608 (1961) (opinion of the Chief Justice) (dictum).

[61] Cases cited note 11 *supra.*

ducted by churches can readily be brought under the familiar statutory exemptions for educational and charitable purposes. While it may be said that these exemptions are an aid to churches and religious corporations, their constitutionality seems validly premised on the fact that they advance legitimate secular purposes and that their benefit to religion is only incidental.

Different considerations apply when the exemption involves a house of worship, whether it is exempt as such or exempt as part of the general property used for religious purposes. Here the exemption benefits an activity which is distinctly religious in character and in which, by hypothesis, the state cannot engage. Government cannot constitutionally spend money to build and operate houses of worship or to promote religious faith and worship, whether on a preferential basis or not. This much seems clear. The argument that the tax exemption is in recognition of a financial savings to the state, therefore, has no relevancy. Nor is it a valid argument to say that the benefit to religion is incidental, since this exemption does benefit religious activity as such. The question raised, then, is whether such an indirect benefit, arising from a grant of tax immunity, stands in any better position than a direct grant of money for this purpose. Certainly the constitutional practice of the states supports the validity of a distinction between tax exemptions and grants of tax funds. Many state constitutions expressly authorize exemptions of property used for worship or other religious purposes while at the same time expressly prohibiting use of tax funds in aid of sectarian purposes.[62] It is evidently the theory of these constitutions that tax exemptions are consistent with the no-aid principle.

It is frequently argued that tax exemptions for a house of worship recognize that religious worship and the cultivation of religious faith result in public benefits through the promotion of morality and good citizenship. Thus, state constitutional practice observes a distinction between public benefits for which tax exemptions may be granted and public purposes for which tax

[62] See constitutions cited notes 2 and 17 *supra*.

funds can be spent. Closely related to this, it seems to me, is the idea that government, in recognition of the place in our pluralistic system of private, voluntary, and non-profit enterprises that serve purposes consistent with the public interest, may appropriately relieve them of obligations otherwise imposed by law in order to further their freedom to operate. With respect to religious activities, we may add that such exemptions help implement the express guarantee of religious liberty, even though such exemptions are not constitutionally required. Hence, it can be argued that the same principle which supports exemption on religious grounds from military service or from Sunday-closing requirements can logically be extended to exempt religious activities from the obligations imposed by tax laws.

Indeed, the Supreme Court has recognized that the government may withhold or condition its coercive power to aid what it considers worthy religious programs, even though it is not required to do so by the free-exercise clause and even though direct financial grants in support of such purposes would be invalid under the non-establishment clause. Probably the most notable instance is the *Zorach* case, where the state exempted children from the usual obligations of the public school program in order to permit them to attend classes for religious instruction. This was a case where, as Justice Douglas said, the state was accommodating its program to the religious needs of its people. Similarly, tax exemptions may be viewed as an accommodation by the state to the place of religion in the life of the individual and the community.

Before concluding I should point out that our problem would in many respects be a simple one if the Supreme Court were to adopt Professor Kurland's thesis that the First Amendment's religion clauses state a special principle of classification, namely, that government can do nothing to hinder or benefit religion as such.[63] According to this analysis, exemptions designed only to benefit churches or religious purposes would be unconstitutional, but exemptions for auxiliary church enterprises such as schools, col-

---

[63] KURLAND, *op. cit. supra* note 25, at 17–18, 111–12.

leges, and hospitals would be valid if these resulted from exemption classifications stated in terms of educational and charitable purposes. It is possible also, as I understand his thesis, that exemptions for religious purposes would be valid if they arose under a broad statute exempting all non-profit organizations coming within the familiar charitable trust concept, including those serving educational and charitable as well as religious purposes.[64]

In concluding let me venture my personal opinion that the Supreme Court, if and when it definitively faces the question of tax exemptions for churches and religious purposes, will not find them unconstitutional. While these exemptions do at first appear to transgress the no-aid-to-religion limitation that the Court has written into the First Amendment and made applicable to the states, I have suggested that the no-aid principle cannot be taken literally and I have indicated possible arguments that may be used to support these exemptions. These arguments are by no means conclusive or compelling, and certainly they will not persuade the absolutist or strict separationist. But at the very least it is true, as the Rhode Island Supreme Court has said, that nothing actually held by the Supreme Court to date compels the conclusion that tax exemptions for religious purposes are unconstitutional.[65] Hovering over the whole question is the long-established history of tax exemptions for churches. Conceding that some of the historical reasons for these exemptions are no longer relevant, I think it is a fair proposition that this history affords a practical construction of the separation principle which is more persuasive than any construction which forces the Court to disregard this historical experience.

Perhaps the Court, in dismissing the appeals in the California and Rhode Island cases[66] as not raising substantial questions, has

---

[64] See Reynolds v. Nusbaum, 17 Wis.2d 148, 157, 115 N.W.2d 761, 766 (1962), which discusses Professor Kurland's thesis and so interprets it with respect to tax exemptions.

[65] See note 43 *supra* and accompanying text.

[66] Cases cited notes 39 and 40 *supra*.

already given us the answer. Its actions may indicate that with respect to this question it is disposed to accept Holmes's axiom that a page of history is worth a volume of logic,[67] as well as Justice Reed's observation that "devotion to the great principle of religious liberty should not lead us [the Court] into a rigid interpretation of the constitutional guarantee that conflicts with accepted habits of our people."[68]

[67] New York Trust Co. v. Eisner, 256 U.S. 345, 349 (1921).

[68] McCollum v. Board of Education, 333 U.S. 203, 256 (1948) (dissenting opinion).

MONRAD G. PAULSEN

Constitutional Problems of
Utilizing a Religious Factor
in Adoptions and
Placements of Children

In America the religious education of children is the business of parents, not of government.[1] Parents (or those *in loco parentis*) determine the amount and kind of religious training that a youngster is to receive, and the legal system does not interfere with that determination save in the most exceptional circumstances. Thus, when the New York Court of Appeals was asked to declare a child "neglected" because her mother was not raising her as a Jew even though the child's paternal ancestors were Jewish, the court replied: "As to the mother's failure to train the little girl in the

MONRAD G. PAULSEN is Professor of Law, Columbia University Law School.

[1] The subject matter of this essay has received treatment several times previously. See Overton, *Religion and Adoption*, 23 TENN. L. REV. 951 (1955); Pfeffer, *Religion in the Upbringing of Children*, 35 B.U.L. REV. 333 (1955); Ramsey, *The Legal Imputation of Religion to an Infant in Adoption Proceedings*, 34 N.Y.U.L. REV. 649 (1959); *Religion in Adoption and Custody*, VILLANOVA INSTITUTE OF CHURCH AND STATE CONFERENCE PROCEEDINGS, 56–114 (1957). Note, 54 COLUM. L. REV. 376 (1954); Note, 64 YALE L.J. 772 (1955).

faith of her fathers, that . . . is within the parent's sole control."[2]
Of course the child's own religious preference must be recognized
at some point in time, a fact the New York Court of Appeals
recognized in another case by giving effect to the choice of a
twelve-year-old.[3] The problems discussed in this paper only arise
when the child is so young that independent choice is not appropriate and the state is called upon to make a decision respecting
the course of a child's upbringing. For such cases it is necessary
to formulate some standards to govern the role of the religious
factor.

THE SUBSTANCE OF THE PARENT'S RIGHT

The United States Constitution protects a parent's choice concerning religious training in at least two ways. First, the principle of
church-state separation requires that government not undertake
religious instruction. Second, a constitutional principle formulated
by the Supreme Court recognizes the right of parents, within
certain limits, to control the instruction of their children in respect to any subject matter. In a dictum in *Pierce v. Society of
Sisters*,[4] the Court said: "The child is not the mere creature of
the State; those who nurture him and direct his destiny have the
right, coupled with the high duty, to recognize and prepare him
for additional obligations."[5] *Pierce* had been preceded by *Meyer
v. Nebraska*,[6] which had decided that a state could not convict a
teacher for giving parochial school instruction in the German
language. The Court protected the teacher's "right thus to teach
and the right of the parents to engage him so to instruct their
children. . . ."[7] The state's authority to direct the education of
the young was held to be qualified by a primary parental power
to control their children's education. "That the State may do

---

[2] Portnoy v. Strasser, 303 N.Y. 539, 544, 104 N.E.2d 895, 898 (1952). The
classic article is Friedman, *The Parental Right to Control the Religious
Education of a Child*, 29 HARV. L. REV. 485 (1916).

[3] Martin v. Martin, 308 N.Y. 136, 123 N.E.2d 812 (1954).

[4] 268 U.S. 510 (1925).   [6] 262 U.S. 390 (1923).

[5] *Id.* at 535.   [7] *Id.* at 400.

much, go very far, indeed, in order to improve the quality of its citizens, physically, mentally and morally, is clear;" the opinion in *Meyer* declared, "but the individual has certain fundamental rights which must be respected."[8] Later, in *Prince v. Massachusetts*,[9] Mr. Justice Rutledge wrote of "the rights of children to exercise their religion, and of parents to give them religious training and to encourage them in the practice of religious belief. . . ."[10]

Since the United States Supreme Court rarely reviews the merits of a decision on child custody, one must look to state courts for the principal opinions that elucidate constitutional rights in this area. As the introductory quotation from the New York Court of Appeals suggests, the substance of the parental right to direct the spiritual training of the child is jealously guarded by state tribunals.

The religious instruction designated by a parent may be quite unusual, and yet the choice will not be disturbed by the state. In a well-known Illinois case, the uncle of a twelve-year-old sought to substitute a state-appointed guardian for the boy's mother on the ground that she was an "improper guardian and wholly unable to care for, protect, train, and educate" the youth.[11] The gravamen of the complaint was that the widowed mother had become a member of the Mazdaznan religion and a fanatic follower and close acquaintance of its leader, one Otoman Zar-Adusht Hanish. The Court held that guardians would be named where a child was being exposed to immorality and vice but that the statute "should not be held to extend to cases where there is merely a difference of opinion as to the best course to pursue in rearing a child."[12] Relief was denied for lack of evidence that the Mazdaznan religion was an immoral religion or that Hanish was an immoral man.

A similar issue arose in an unusual New York case where a wife who was residing with her husband in apparent marital harmony except for the religious issue sought to obtain sole custody

---

[8] *Id.* at 401.   [9] 321 U.S. 158 (1944).   [10] *Id.* at 165.

[11] Lindsay v. Lindsay, 257 Ill. 328, 330, 100 N.E. 892, 893 (1913).

[12] *Id.* at 340, 100 N.E. at 897.

of a nine-year-old daughter in order to direct her religious education.[13] The wife's petition charged that her husband had recently become a votary of the Megiddo cult and that as a consequence was teaching the child the theories and beliefs of Megiddo (including the belief that the first person who teaches a child Megiddo is the child's mother), keeping her away from home about a quarter of the time, and causing her to be dressed in unfashionable wearing apparel—all with the effect of producing queerness, bigotry, and fanaticism in the child. The Appellate Division preserved the joint custody of the parents but entered an order limiting the father's right to take the child from the home for lengthy periods. The Court of Appeals reversed and ordered dismissal of the proceeding, declaring:

> Dispute between parents when it does not involve anything immoral or harmful to the welfare of the child is beyond the reach of the law. . . . No end of difficulties would arise should judges try to tell parents how to bring up their children. Only when moral, mental, and physical conditions are so bad as seriously to affect the health or morals of children should the courts be called upon to act.[14]

The foregoing decisions protect the choices of parents, but some language in the opinions suggests that parental freedom to involve children in religious practices and to choose their religious education is not unbounded.

If a parent's religious commitment interferes with his capacity or willingness to provide the proper temporal care for a child he may be denied custody, not because of religion but for related reasons having a sound secular basis. This was the principle the court sought to apply in an 1848 Ohio case where a father, who had become a member of the community of Shakers, sought custody of his two daughters after his wife's death.[15] The Court denied the father custody of the children because his avowed purpose was to take them to the common-property community of the

---

[13] Sisson v. Sisson, 246 App. Div. 151, 285 N.Y.S. 41 (1936), *rev'd*, 271 N.Y. 285, 2 N.E.2d 660 (1936).

[14] 271 N.Y. at 287–88, 2 N.E.2d at 661.

[15] Ball v. Hand, 1 Ohio Dec. Reprint 238 (1848).

Shakers, where (since Shakers allegedly abjured all natural affection and denounced the marriage and parent-child relation) their care and education would be turned over to "female care-takers." This, the court felt, suggested that the father had "a morbid state of the amative and philoprogenitive faculties, bordering on insanity, and totally inconsistent with a rational discharge of parental duty."[16] Similarly, where a child's life has been in serious danger because his parents refused on religious grounds to provide him with necessary medical care, several courts have sanctioned the temporary withdrawal of custody from the parents and the appointment of a special guardian who will obtain the necessary medical care.[17]

Instances of state interference with the parental right to direct the child's religious education and belief are understandably rare. A prominent example is a recent Utah case where the neglect and dependency jurisdiction of the juvenile court was invoked against members of a sect engaged in preaching and practicing polygamy.[18] The father had been living in a polygamous relationship with three wives, by whom he had a total of twenty-six children. When the law-enforcement officers made a raid on Short Creek, an isolated community straddling the Utah-Arizona border, the father was arrested, and the Utah Department of Public Welfare promptly began neglect proceedings on behalf of eight minor children of the second wife, ranging from two to seventeen years of age. Thereafter the juvenile court adjudicated the children neglected and placed them in the custody of the Department of Public Welfare—with the provision that they might remain in the home of their mother if the parents would comply with the law prohibiting polygamous cohabitation and would promise to counsel, encourage, and advise the children to observe and not to violate the Utah laws relating to marriage and sexual offenses, notwithstand-

16 *Id.* at 244.

17 *E.g.,* People v. Labrenz, 411 Ill. 618, 104 N.E.2d 769 (1952), *cert. denied,* 344 U.S. 824 (1952); State v. Perricone, 37 N.J. 463, 181 A.2d 751 (1962).

18 *In re* Black, 3 Utah 2d 315, 283 P.2d 887 (1955).

ing any religious doctrines to the contrary. When the parents refused to accept these conditions, the juvenile court ordered the children into the custody of the Department. The parents appealed, urging that the court's decree violated their constitutional rights by attempting to "force them to desist from their beliefs" and that it "deprives them of their right to teach their children the religious beliefs to which they adhere."[19] Their belief, succinctly summarized in the lower court's finding, was "that there is a law of God requiring men to take and live with more than one wife and that failure to do so constitutes a breach of religious duties."[20]

The Utah Supreme Court was unanimous in affirming the judgment of the juvenile court, but there was no unanimity in its opinions. One justice took no part, one concurred in the result without opinion, and each of the other three filed his own separate opinion. The principal opinion in terms of length was bitterly condemnatory, as this short excerpt reveals:

They have not only failed to teach their children that polygamy and unlawful cohabitation are against the law and morals, but they have positively taught their children that the law of plural marriage and the practice of plural marriage was right and they have encouraged their children to teach, preach and practice it. Further, these appellants have actually practiced plural marriage and have unlawfully cohabited in the presence of these children. They have done further than to advocate the correctness of plural marriage, they have provided the horrible example to these children and have subjected the children to living with the system.[21]

The second opinion went directly to the point that the appellants' actions had to be governed by the "laws of our state," which they had obdurately refused to observe. Since the court could not permit some citizens immunity from the law by reason of their special knowledge of the "law of God," this opinion concluded that the trial court had no choice other than to enter the order in ques-

---

19 *Id.* at 334, 283 P.2d at 901.

20 *Id.* at 320, 283 P.2d at 891. (Partly italicized in original.)

21 *Id.* at 346, 283 P.2d at 909.

tion.[22] The third opinion, that of Justice Henroid, is short enough and pertinent enough, to be set forth in substantially complete text.

I concur. In doing so, however I reserve my opinion on all matters touched upon in the main opinion not directly related to the legal aspects of the case. For example, I cannot say, as the main opinion seems to imply, that polygamy is *morally* wrong. It is neither morally nor legally wrong in Turkey and elsewhere. It is questionable whether it was morally or legally wrong in Utah Territory in the 19th Century, and I like to think, at least, that my great grandfather was not only a law-abiding citizen, but was not immoral according to the mores of his time. What is moral, or legal, depends in most part upon time, place and circumstance. Today, in Utah, the circumstances which go to make up adultery and polygamy, legislatively are considered and treated as felonies,—both of which offenses have been committed by the father in this case. Our decision, therefore, can be resolved by answering a most simple question: Do the statutes of our state constitutionally permit the Juvenile Court to deprive parents of the custody of their children, if such parents practice and teach their children to practice a felony,—*any* felony? This question must be answered in the affirmative, and there would be little difficulty in answering it if the felony being taught to the children were murder, rape, armed robbery, burglary and the like. Where children and parents and religion are involved, the answer to the question tends to stick in our throats, but we are duty bound to utter it when confronted with it.[23]

In summary, it is right to say that parents are permitted under the law to teach their children any religious and spiritual doctrine, even one that is strange, unusual, or bizarre. However, parents must not allow their religious practices to interfere with providing proper temporal care for their children, and they have no legal right to teach their children to commit criminal acts even though that teaching may be defended on the ground that it is merely a teaching of religious truth.

When a husband and wife cease to live together, the right to control the child's religious upbringing normally passes to the

[22] *Id.* at 352–53, 283 P.2d at 913–14.

[23] *Id.* at 353, 283 P.2d at 914.

parent or other individual in whose custody the child has been placed.[24] This is a subject that often gives rise to bitter controversy, but it is one with which the state and its courts are understandably reluctant to interfere. One expression of this reluctance lies in the general rule that agreements between parents respecting the religious upbringing of children are not enforced by the courts should the parents separate.[25] The opinions reaching that result have given a number of reasons: (1) the contracts in question seek to affect a parental right which cannot be the subject of a contract; (2) the Constitution forbids the enforcement of the contract; (3) the agreements are vague; and (4) the supervision of such decrees is beyond judicial competence. The last reason is especially persuasive. Obviously law is a clumsy instrument with which to control the most subtle aspects of human conduct. Only rather gross behavior, or states of mind which can be evidenced by overt behavior, can conveniently be the subject of legal inquiry in a courtroom. If a mother were to be held to an agreement to raise her child as a Catholic, for example, the courts could readily determine whether she sent the child to Mass or to a parochial school but could not successfully look into the home and see the reality of day-to-day religious instruction by word and example.[26]

It is of course very difficult for a court to avoid the religious factor when parents of different faiths bring the subject into a controversy over who shall be awarded custody of the children.[27] Some of the pitfalls in this subject are suggested by a 1957 Kansas case where a trial court ordered a mother to relinquish custody

[24] The custodian's choice is generally respected even against a parent, although in one recorded instance a parent not having custody succeeded in obtaining a court order that the custodian give his child certain religious training. Lemke v. Guthmann, 105 Neb. 251, 181 N.W. 132 (1920).

[25] See Note, 59 Colum. L. Rev. 680 n.2 (1959).

[26] The opinion in Lynch v. Uhlenhopp, 248 Iowa 68, 78 N.W.2d 491 (1956), is especially instructive on this point.

[27] A collection of the case law is found in *Religion as a Factor in Awarding Custody of Child*, 66 A.L.R.2d 1410 (1959).

of the couple's three children to the father. The most prominent allegation in the father's motion was the claim that he should have custody because his wife was a member of Jehovah's Witnesses and because "by subjecting the children to such teachings, they will tend to become overtired and emotionally upset, and . . . . will be brought up in a manner that will tend to make them unpatriotic citizens of the United States. . . ."[28] The subject of these claims also figured prominently in the oral testimony and in the court's findings. On appeal, the Kansas Supreme Court set aside the new custody order on the ground that the lower court had abused its discretion by allowing the matter of religion to become an integral part of its determination of the matter.

In a Pennsylvania case, on the other hand, a father succeeded in winning his five-year-old daughter's custody away from his estranged wife solely for reasons relating to her activities as a Jehovah's Witness.[29] Relying on evidence that the mother was taking the child out from door to door and from street corner to street corner distributing literature, the court observed:

If this mother wishes to inculcate in the mind of her child doctrines and rules of conduct at variance with those of the vast majority of children with whom she will associate in life, we presume that is her right, but when she carries her activities to the point where in our opinion the health and well-being of her child are injured, then the court should step in to protect what we consider the best interests and permanent welfare of the child.[30]

Similarly, the court may take notice of the religion of the party having custody in making special provisions to safeguard the temporal welfare of the child. For example, a New York court imposed a requirement that a child in the custody of a mother who was a Christian Scientist be given regular medical care.[31]

[28] Jackson v. Jackson, 181 Kan. 1, 5, 309 P.2d 705, 708 (1957).

[29] Kaufmann v. Kaufmann, 69 Montg.Co.L.R. 292 (Pa. C.P. 1953).

[30] *Id.* at 295. *Accord,* Prince v. Massachusetts, 321 U.S. 158 (1944).

[31] Gluckstern v. Gluckstern, 158 N.Y.S.2d 504 (Sup. Ct. 1956), *aff'd* 3 App. Div. 2d 999, 165 N.Y.S.2d 432 (1956) *aff'd* 4 N.Y.2d 521, 151 N.E.2d 897, 176 N.Y.S.2d 352 (1956).

THE RELIGIOUS CRITERIA IN CHILD PLACEMENTS

The principal problems regarding the role of religion in relation to the custody of children have arisen under legislation setting up religious criteria to guide the child-placement decisions of courts and social welfare agencies. In considering this legislation it is well to note the contrast between adoption proceedings, which normally fix the circumstances of a youngster's childhood with permanency, and other kinds of placement, which often make dispositions that are merely temporary. This difference is important in assessing the constitutionality of different types of legislation.

The statutes under which courts and social agencies act in respect to probation, foster-home placement, guardianship, and juvenile court commitments contemplate a transitory situation. Youngsters ultimately are discharged from probation, released from institutions, and reclaimed by parents. Not only does time change these placement situations, but the decisions of agencies and courts themselves are subject to change at any time. It is true that "temporary" placements (especially those to foster homes) sometimes turn out in fact to be permanent, but the arrangements are designed to meet a temporary situation and must be judged with that purpose in mind. The continuity of religious experience upon which the laws under discussion insist is widely held to be psychologically beneficial both to the child and to his family. In addition, the non-adoption situations usually involve an older group of children who have been exposed to some religious teaching. If the state failed to provide a way for nurturing these youngsters' personal religious commitments during the period that they are subjected to the control of government, the most serious questions of impairment of religious freedom would arise.

The statutes concerning non-adoptive placements are of great variety, but they generally respond to the foregoing considerations by making some provision for preserving the child's existing religious affiliation. For example, it is common to provide that probation, commitment, or placement dispositions by the juvenile court are to be made in accordance with the religion of the youngster. The New York Family Court Act states that whenever a child is committed by the Family Court to any authorized association, agency, society, or institution, other than a state institution, the commitment must be made "when practicable, to a duly authorized association, agency, society or institution under the control of persons of the same religious faith or persuasion as that of the child."[32] Furthermore, another section of this Act requires that "when there is a sufficient number of probation officers of the same religious faith as that of the child to be placed on probation, the child shall be placed on probation with a probation officer of the same religious faith as that of the child."[33] In still another place the Act provides that the Family Court may enter orders to protect children against aggressive behavior by their parents or custodian, but in so doing the court must "insure that in the care, protection, discipline and guardianship of the child his religious faith shall be preserved and protected."[34]

One disadvantage of legislative insistence on giving overriding weight to a religious factor in temporary placement is that this may put a court probation officer or an agency social worker to a choice that seems unwise. For example, the foster home with the greatest advantage for a child may not possess the same religious background. Hence, the choice of that home would be impossible.

One can agree that "religious factor" provisions are undesirable as a matter of legislative policy and yet assert that they are constitutional. The position embraced in this paper is, as we shall argue more fully below, that when the state acts to sustain and reinforce the religious choice of a youngster or his parents, the federal constitution permits it to make decisions which react to religious factors.

The adoption laws have produced the most difficult constitutional questions about the use of the religious factor. Here, too, the statutes exhibit a great variation. Some laws merely provide for a notation of the religion of the child and of the adoptive

[32] N.Y. FAMILY CT. ACT § 116(a).

[33] N.Y. FAMILY CT. ACT § 252(c).

[34] N.Y. FAMILY CT. ACT § 759(e).

parents on the petition for adoption.[35] Others authorize or require an investigating social agency to report to a court prior to an adoption concerning the religious background of both the young-ster to be adopted and his proposed adoptive parents.[36] Typically these statutes expressly authorize a court to take religion into account as one factor to be considered when that court makes the ultimate decision in an adoption or custody matter. Finally, some legislation provides that the religious factor is to be substantially determinative of the result. These laws have put the constitutional issue most sharply.

Three of the states that give courts explicit instructions to match the religion of adoptive children and adoptive parents are New York,[37] Illinois,[38] and Massachusetts.[39] In New York and Massachusetts an adoption must match religion "when practi-cable"; in Illinois, "whenever possible." Each statute has pro-duced litigation which found its way into the highest state court.

A 1957 case, *Cooper v. Hinrichs*,[40] construed the Illinois statute to permit the exercise of discretion by a trial court which decides upon an adoption. The use of the words, "whenever possible," the Supreme Court of Illinois said, "does suggest that the legisla-ture contemplated that identity of religion between adopting par-ents and children would not be followed in all adoptions."[41] The court also pointed to the word "shall," which preceded the phrase "whenever possible" in the statute, and noted that courts had construed this word in reading other laws to mean "may" rather than "must." The Illinois court did insist that religion be given greater significance than other factors. Its opinion saw a legislative intention to stress the religious factor and to direct a preference

---

[35] *E.g.*, Iowa Code Ann. § 600.1 (1950).

[36] *E.g.*, Colo. Rev. Stat. 4–1–7(1) (e) (1953).

[37] N.Y. Family Ct. Act § 116.

[38] Ill. Rev. Stat. ch. 4, § 9.1–15 (1961).

[39] Mass. Ann. Laws ch. 210, § 5B (1955).

[40] 10 Ill.2d 269, 140 N.E.2d 293 (1957).

[41] *Id.* at 273, 140 N.E.2d at 295.

for persons of the same religion as the child to be adopted when they are otherwise qualified to promote the welfare of the child.

Such a construction pays respect to the desire of the natural parents that their child will be accorded the benefits which they believe are afforded by the particular religion they profess, and at the same time does not allow this potential benefit to jeopardize the welfare of the child or be at the expense of the child's best interests.[42]

The case was returned to the trial court to determine whether the adoption would in fact promote the best interests of the children, in view of the difference in religion between them and the adopting parents.

Similarly, the New York Court of Appeals in 1958 held that the phrase "when practicable" did not bind trial courts to the religious factor in every case.[43] Judge Fuld wrote that the New York law

contains no absolute requirement that the faith of the foster parents be that of the child. The statute calls upon the court to give custody to persons of the same religious faith as that of the child "when practicable." That term is of broad content, necessarily designed to accord the trial judge a discretion to approve as adoptive parents persons of a faith different from the child's in exceptional situations.[44]

The legislature in New York responded to this decision by enacting certain provisions in the New York Family Court Act. Effective September 1, 1962, this Act contains a legislative declaration that the religious protection provisions of the Act, which are very extensive, "shall be interpreted literally, so as to assure that in the care, protection, guardianship, discipline or control of any child his religious faith shall be preserved and protected by the court."[45] In addition, the words "when practicable" are not to be given effect by the court if "there is a proper . . . person of the same religious faith or persuasion as that of the child available"

[42] *Id.* at 276, 140 N.E.2d at 297.

[43] Matter of Maxwell, 4 N.Y.2d 429, 151 N.E.2d 848 (1958).

[44] *Id.* at 434, 151 N.E.2d at 850.

[45] N.Y. FAMILY CT. ACT § 116(d).

as guardian, custodian, or adoptive parent.[46] Furthermore, "when practicable" permits no latitude in the case of institutional commitment or placement if there is an institution under the control of persons of the same religion as that of the child available to receive the child. Finally, the law requires that a judge who makes commitments, placements, or adoption orders across religious lines, "shall state or recite the facts which impel it to make such disposition."[47] One would not now anticipate many cases of non-matching adoptions to take place in New York.

In a Massachusetts opinion, *Petitions of Goldman*,[48] the phrase "when practicable" was given a judicial interpretation which produced a result substantially similar to that reached by the New York legislation. In that case Jewish parents sought to adopt eight-month-old twins who had been living with them since they were about two weeks old. Petitioners were possessed of a good home, had adequate means, and had given the children adequate care and affection. The trial judge found the petitioning couple well equipped financially and physically to bring up the children and held that they had treated the children as their own. The mother and "the natural father" were Catholics—at least the mother *had been* a practicing Catholic—but she had fallen away from the church as far as religious participation was concerned. She had consented in writing to the Goldmans' adoption petition and she had stated that she knew they were Jewish and was satisfied that the twins be raised in the Jewish faith. Lynn, Massachusetts, a city near the petitioners' residence, included many fine Catholic couples who had filed applications with the Catholic Charities Bureau seeking to adopt Catholic children like the Goldman twins. The trial judge found that these prospective parents would be able to give the children the same material and emotional care offered by the Jewish parents. He therefore con-

---

[46] N.Y. FAMILY CT. ACT § 116(e).

[47] N.Y. FAMILY CT. ACT § 116(f).

[48] 331 Mass. 647, 121 N.E.2d 843 (1954), *cert. denied*, 348 U.S. 942 (1955).

cluded that "it would not be for the best interests of the twins to decree adoptions in these cases."[49]

The Supreme Judicial Court of Massachusetts accepted the trial court findings and affirmed its decree. The court brushed aside the argument that the statute, as interpreted in *Goldman*, was unconstitutional either as a law respecting an establishment of religion or a prohibition of free exercise of religious faith:

All religions are treated alike. There is no "subordination" of one sect to another. No burden is placed upon anyone for maintenance of any religion. No exercise of religion is required, prevented, or hampered. It is argued that there is interference with the mother's right to determine the religion of her offspring, and that in these cases she has determined it shall be Jewish. Passing the point that so far as concerns religion she seems to have consented rather than commanded and seems to have been "interested only that the babies were in a good home," there is clearly no interference with any wish of hers as long as she retains her status as a parent.[50]

The Court avoided any pronouncements on the most difficult point in this case: "the philosophy underlying the concept that a child too young to understand any religion, even imperfectly, nevertheless may have a religion."[51] (The Goldman children had not been baptized.) This intriguing question was judged to be foreclosed by the statutory provision that the religious faith of the child is identical with the religious faith of the parents, or in the case of dispute, the faith of the mother. "The principle that children should, in general, be adopted within the faith of their natural parents," the opinion said, "has received widespread approval."[52]

The Supreme Court of the United States declined to review *Goldman*.[53] It is of course dangerous to guess reasons for a denial of certiorari, but it may be significant that the church-state issue in *Goldman* was to some extent blunted by the fact that the trial judge had been unable to satisfy himself concerning the manner

[49] *Id.* at 648, 121 N.E.2d at 844.

[50] *Id.* at 652, 121 N.E.2d at 846.   [52] *Id.* at 653, 121 N.E.2d at 846.

[51] *Ibid.*   [53] 348 U.S. 942 (1955).

in which the twins had come into the home of the petitioners. The appellate court's opinion observes that "the judge may well have doubted whether all the circumstances had been revealed and whether the requirements of the law . . . had been fully observed."[54]

The statutes discussed above give special weight to the factor of religion. Other statutes and administrative practices, which merely provide that religion is to be taken into account along with other factors in an adoption or custody matter, can present the same kind of problem. Thus, it is possible to imagine a case in which two prospective custodians or proposed adoptive parents have equal qualifications. If religion is considered in such a case and serves to tip the balance so that the adults who are of the same religion as the child are awarded custody, a benefit has in fact been bestowed by reason of religion.

Religion is employed as a criterion in adoption and child-placement cases even where statutes do not require it. Judges, agencies, and agency personnel are likely to match children and prospective custodians on a religious basis.[55] A New York City practice respecting religion and custody is interesting. Foundling children, whose religious heritage is unknown, are placed alternately with Catholic, Protestant, and Jewish social agencies on a rotating basis.[56] Thus, children receive their religious affiliation by lot. Agencies normally will not give children to atheists and avowed agnostics for the purpose of adoption. Where the husband and wife are of mixed faiths, they have little chance of getting a child. Because relatively few Jewish women give birth out of wedlock, compared with Catholic and Protestant women, childless Jewish couples have great trouble in effecting adoptions. Similar problems are doubtless faced by ethical culturalists, Mormons, and other members of recognized separate denominations.

Groups which are strongly committed to the separation prin-

[54] Petitions of Goldman, *supra* note 48, at 650, 121 N.E.2d at 844.

[55] See Broeder and Barrett, *Impact of Religious Factors in Nebraska Adoptions*, 38 NEB. L. REV. 641 (1959).

[56] Wicklein, *Religion as a Factor in Adoption Administration*, N.Y. Times, Oct. 11, 1959, p. 1, col. 2 (city ed.).

ciple condemn the use of a religious factor if it is given anything like a decisive effect. In May, 1962, a Special Committee on Church and State made a recommendation with respect to adoption in its report to the 174th General Assembly of the United Presbyterian Church in the United States of America. "In the light of the separation principle," the report said, "Christians should be deeply concerned about laws which use the power of the state to enforce religious concepts which are not the state's proper concern."[57] The statement continued by urging the Church to:

Consider the adoption of children solely on the basis of the temporal benefit to the child; to the family to which the child is being adopted; and, if necessitated by circumstances, to the family which the child is leaving. Except where demonstrably pertinent to the above test, no consideration of race, creed, color, status, or economic circumstances should enter into the process of adoption either through restrictive laws or by discriminatory exercise of discretion by judges.[58]

THE CONSTITUTIONAL ISSUES

Statutes, judicial decisions, and practices of the sort discussed in the preceding section put a serious constitutional issue: Does use of a religious test in custody or adoption matters violate the principle of church-state separation? We can begin this inquiry by examining the objectives of religious matching.

One possible goal of religious matching is to help a church or a synagogue retain "its own." (A religious organization is likely to regard offspring of the faithful as part of its group.) This aim, however, is hardly a proper one for government under the Constitution. Governmental action taken to strengthen religious bodies as such is certainly barred by the First Amendment. If the state may not support churches by giving them a place for the religious training of children or by causing a prayer to be composed and

[57] *Relations Between Church and State* 18 (A Report to the 174th General Assembly of the United Presbyterian Church in the United States of America, May, 1962).

[58] *Ibid.*

recited in school every day, it is also barred from a program of church-membership maintenance.

Matching may have the aim of benefiting the child (and perhaps the state) by obtaining religious training for him to aid his growth as a moral agent and a good citizen. In spite of some evidence to the contrary,[59] it is widely held that religious training produces personal and civic virtue. Eight reflective thinkers, writing for the Center for the Study of Democratic Institutions, concluded:

> We have said that religion serves the causes of freedom by insisting on the unfathomable depths of the human personality, by proposing and nurturing the moral ideals and ethical standards society lives by, by reenforcing the sense of personal dignity that sustains freedom, and by forming men of virtue who can take their place as citizens in a society whose freedom ultimately depends on the exercise of virtue.[60]

If the state does adopt the goal of sensitizing a child to religion, the state would then have to choose some particular religious contact for him. It could be argued with some force that the state can choose the religion of the child's parental background because the state, under the Constitution, has no other way of making a choice of religion except by lot. For state officials to make the choice they might think best would be for the officials to judge the comparative worth of religious groups. Surely the separation principle bars such judgments.

Some may insist that *Everson v. Board of Education*,[61] the school-bus case, is helpful to sustain religious-matching statutes on the theory that a child's moral training may be thus advanced. In *Everson* a New Jersey school district was permitted to pay for bus transportation to a private school—indeed, in that case, to a Catholic parochial school. The expenditure was justified on the

---

[59] See Broeder and Barrett, *supra* note 55, at 669–71.

[60] RELIGION AND AMERICAN SOCIETY 34 (Center for the Study of Democratic Institutions 1961). See also Article III of the Northwest Ordinance of 1787: "Religion, morality and knowledge being necessary to good government and the happiness of mankind, schools and the means of education shall forever be encouraged." 1 Stat. 50, 51-52 n.(*a*) (1789).

[61] 330 U.S. 1 (1947).

ground that the safety provided by bus travel to school was the aim of a public welfare program for children. The secular aim— the safety of youth—could be pursued, although religious institutions might benefit incidentally. A legislature, the argument runs, in making provision for "the best interests of the child" might judge that religious training is necessary to form good character.

Such a resolution of the constitutional issue is almost certainly unsound. In *Everson* itself the opinion of the Court said that government cannot "influence a person to go to or remain away from church."[62] Mr. Justice Black in *McCollum v. Board of Education*,[63] the first of the two "released-time" cases before the Supreme Court of the United States, spoke against the utilization of a "public school system to aid any or all religious faiths or sects in the dissemination of their doctrines and *ideals. . . .*"[64] In the second "released-time" case, *Zorach v. Clauson*,[65] the Court, while upholding the New York system of providing time during the regular school day for off-the-premises religious instruction, said that "if it were established that any one or more teachers were using their office to *persuade* or force students to take religious instruction, a wholly different case would be presented."[66] In another place the opinion says flatly: "Government may not . . . undertake religious instruction."[67] Thus, the language in these cases suggests that the state itself may not constitutionally embark upon a program of religious education, even if the legislature were to decide that children would benefit morally from the program. The authority of this language is strengthened by the school-prayer case, which forbade the daily recitation of a state-composed prayer in the public schools although the prayer had been recommended by the New York State Board of Regents and published as a part of its "Statement on Moral and Spiritual Training in the Schools."[68] The First Amendment thus forbids the government to build character by means of religious training.

[62] *Id.* at 15.

[63] 333 U.S. 203 (1948).

[64] *Id.* at 211. (Emphasis added.)

[65] 343 U.S. 306 (1952).

[66] *Id.* at 311. (Emphasis added.)

[67] *Id.* at 314.

[68] Engel v. Vitale, 370 U.S. 421, 423 (1962).

A collateral effect, if not purpose, of the matching requirement is that of impeding proselytizing by state officers. Indeed, the New York law requiring a child to be placed in accordance with his religion was passed when accusations that the Children's Aid Society, a Protestant group, was placing many Catholic children in Protestant homes "gave rise to a countermovement aimed toward placing dependent, neglected, and delinquent children of Catholic parentage in Catholic homes or instituitons."[69]

Although the cases speaking to the separation principle do not permit the state to use religion as a criterion when making placement and adoption decisions if it does so for the purpose of helping the church or for the purpose of helping a child achieve virtue by giving him religious training, there are two other possible aims to be reviewed: (1) helping a child retain his personal faith while he is under the supervision of the state, and (2) carrying out the wishes of parents. Whether a state may serve either of these objectives is, I submit, an open question under the existing opinions.

1. A youngster who has some personal religious faith has a claim on the state which a newborn infant does not. Thirteen- or fourteen-year-olds have sufficient capacity to choose a religion and hence have the same right as adults to the free exercise of that religion. When the state, for its purposes, asserts control over a child by placement or institutionalization, the youngster ought to have an opportunity to keep his personal religion. Ordinarily the state leaves the problem of obtaining access to religious contact in the private hands of those who wish it, but when the state interjects itself into a life to such a degree that an individual's ordinary freedom of choice concerning behavior is seriously limited, then the state has a duty to provide a way for the person to reach the religious community of his choice. If this principle is sound, state institutions do not violate the establishment clause by providing a place for periodic worship by inmates who choose to participate, and the state can provide chaplains at public expense.

[69] SCHNEIDER, THE HISTORY OF PUBLIC WELFARE IN NEW YORK STATE 1609–1866, 334–35 (1938).

It can also direct that children who are in the hands of the state can be placed with persons and agencies of their own faith. Religion is not established by such arrangements, but rather the right of the person to religious freedom is recognized. The preservation of the child's chosen faith would therefore seem to be a proper objective for the state. This theory would sustain the constitutionality of the application of religious-matching statutes to a large proportion of the non-adoptive placements, as well as to some adoptions.

2. We have seen that parents have a protected right to choose the religion of their children. Often, when natural parents have failed or are unwilling or unable to discharge their normal function, the state must provide a substitute for parental care. Can the state, under these circumstances, constitutionally succeed to the parents' right to make a religious choice for the children?

A father rules, Aristotle reminds us, "by virtue both of love and of the respect due to age." The statement underscores the state's difficulty as it attempts to take on the various aspects of a parental role. The state does not possess power by virtue of the "respect due to age." Its authority does not stem from the need to control the immature. The good state orders a society in a legal and constitutional way seeking justice in the affairs of mature men. The state, as such, cannot really love anyone subject to its powers. It operates, to express the obvious, through salaried agents and institutional forms. The instant constitutional issue is put by asking whether in the choice of agents or institutions the state may make a selection on religious grounds.

The state is a strange parent because it isn't a person at all and because, generally, it is subject to constitutional limitations. Consequently, in America at least, the state could not require that all children whose custody is to be determined in neglect, delinquency, or adoption proceedings be placed in a Catholic or an Episcopal or a Jewish home. The state could not prefer one religion over another, even for the purpose of acting as a parent. Thus, when acting as a substitute parent the state cannot choose a particular religion for its ward on the merits of that religion.

Where the child does not have his own chosen faith, the Constitution, in my view, gives the state two choices. It may ignore the religious factor altogether. Thus, in placing a child, state officials could make assignments to persons or institutions without regard to religion. On the other hand, the state may adopt someone else's determination in regard to religious upbringing. Delaware's statute regarding adoption has clearly expressed this choice:

> No child born out of wedlock shall be placed for adoption unless at least one of the prospective adopting parents shall be of the same religion as the natural mother or of the religion in which she has reared the child or allowed it to be reared. . . .
>
> Should the natural mother in a notarized statement made prior to placement for adoption declare that she is indifferent to the religion in which the child shall be reared, or if the religion of the mother is not known, or there is none, then the authorized agency may make placement without regard to religion.[70]

I submit that in respecting the natural parents' wishes the state does not violate the separation principle but merely reinforces the already accepted fundamental proposition that parents primarily control the religion of the young.[71]

The operation of the statutes requiring religious matching in most instances is consistent with the aims of protecting a child's freedom of religion or of carrying out parental direction. Yet some problems remain. Typically, the statutes are not drafted, as is the Delaware law, expressly to reflect a parent's choice of religious training. They merely provide that the religion of the child match that of the prospective custodian. Those statutes which presume that a child shares the religion of its parents conform to the principle of parental determination because parents are likely to desire that their child be instructed in the faith which the parents themselves accept. By setting up a presumption to that effect

---

[70] DEL. CODE ANN. tit. 13, ch. 9, § 911 (1953).

[71] A vicarious parent ought to have the same right as a parent. If parents have lost their right to raise a child through intentional relinquishment or misconduct and another person acts in their place, the state may follow the directive of the vicarious parent on the subject of religion in making its placement decisions without violating the Constitution.

the statutes attempt to carry out parental wishes so far as they are known. Whether a child's religion, determined by relation to baptism or other form of infant dedication, can be the basis of a constitutional placement decision would depend, in this analysis, upon whether the dedication was an expression of a parent's choice of religion for the child. The surreptitious baptism of an infant by a third person can have significance only within the religious community as a matter of a religious doctrine, and should not be given any official operative effect by the state.

The state may not respond to the claims of religious doctrine in dealing with a child; but it may act to protect the religious choice of the child, and it may attempt to carry out the actual or presumed wishes of the parents. The distinction between this permissible role of the state and the forbidden purpose of prescribing religious training for its own purposes is aptly illustrated by a well-known juvenile court case in which a youngster whom a trial court had adjudicated delinquent was required to attend Sunday school and church each Sunday. The Virginia Supreme Court of Appeals reversed, saying:

No civil authority has the right to require any one to accept or reject any religious belief or to contribute any support thereto. The growth of religion is not made dependent on force or alliance with the state. Its support is left to moral and spiritual forces.[72]

While the state may not require church attendance to build character, can it not assist parents in their attempts to offer religious instruction to their young children? *Zorach v. Clauson*,[73] the second released-time case, suggests an affirmative answer to the question. The New York released-time scheme of religious instruction excuses those pupils whose parents make a proper request that their children be permitted to go to churches and synagogues for religious instruction. Those who leave school and fail to report to the place of instruction violate the school-attendance laws and may be taken before the Family Court.

The state cannot, consistent with the constitutional principle of

[72] Jones v. Commonwealth, 185 Va. 335, 344–45, 38 S.E.2d 444, 448 (1946).
[73] 343 U.S. 306 (1952).

separation, make a choice of religion contrary to the expressed wishes of the parent having custody. Under the principle discussed here, a court cannot constitutionally employ the religious factor if it possesses information negating the presumption that parents desire their children raised in the family religion. Accordingly, the *Goldman* case was decided unconstitutionally. The mother knew of the Goldmans' plan to raise the twins as Jews and was satisfied with it. The court's insistence that the children be given a Roman Catholic upbringing could not have been justified on the ground that the wishes of a parent were being carried out, and in the case of infants there is no other ground that meets the standard of the federal Constitution.

The theme developed here deserves to be tested against Professor Philip B. Kurland's arresting thesis concerning the separation of church and state.[74] Professor Kurland's reading of the cases in the Supreme Court has led him to offer the following formulation:

[T]he proper construction of the religion clauses of the first amendment is that the freedom and separation clauses should be read as a single precept that government cannot utilize religion as a standard for action or inaction because these clauses prohibit classification in terms of religion either to confer a benefit or to impose a burden.[75]

As I understand this thesis, it also requires a judgment that the *Goldman* case was incorrectly decided. The Goldmans were unable to adopt the twins because the Goldmans were Jewish and the children's parents had been Roman Catholic. Surely the inability to adopt certain children is the imposition of a burden, and in *Goldman* the burden was imposed by employing a religious classification not based on the choice of parents. In cases where the aim of religious matching is to carry out parental wishes, the Kurland thesis might not forbid the use of religious criteria. In such instances government is not utilizing "religion as a standard for action or inaction." Rather it is employing a standard of obedience to the wishes of parents. The parents make the choice; the state carries it out.

[74] See KURLAND, RELIGION AND THE LAW (1961).

[75] *Id.* at 18.

CONCLUSION

The principle of separation cannot mean that religion is not to take benefit from state action. The state may see to it that the terms of a will which benefit the Roman Catholic Church are carried out. A trust providing income for the Methodist Church will be supported by the full complement of remedies available for such a purpose. In many instances the state gives scope to private choice.

Religious-matching provisions are constitutional when they seek to uphold the right of a child to gain access to the religion of his choice, or, in the case of those too young to possess a meaningful personal commitment, when they endeavor to maintain the right of a parent to select the religious education of his child. These laws are constitutional in these circumstances because their purpose is to determine religious training with reference to a private rather than a governmental preference.

PHILIP B. KURLAND

The School Prayer Cases

Unlike T. S. Eliot's world, the past two Terms of the United States Supreme Court have ended with a bang, not a whimper. The whimpering came later. The last decision day of the 1961 Term climaxed in a declaration in *Engel v. Vitale*[1] that the Regents' prayer prescribed by the school authorities of the State of New York could not constitutionally be made a part of the state's public education program. The immediate reaction to *Engel* was violent and gross. The press was divided.[2] The divines were also divided, in part along denominational lines. The Catholic hierarchy and its spokesmen were almost unanimous in condemnation of the Court

PHILIP B. KURLAND is Professor of Law, The University of Chicago. Part of this chapter is adapted from the author's article in [1962] SUP. CT. REV. 1.

[1] 370 U.S. 421 (1962).

[2] "[E]ven worse was the sight of so many otherwise responsible newspapers getting completely swept off their feet by the tide of emotionalism." N.Y. Herald Tribune, July 5, 1962, p. 18, col. 3. The press was divided pretty much as one would have anticipated, as shown by the following examples:

In defense of the Court: New York Times, New York Herald Tribune, New York Post, Pittsburgh Post-Gazette, Hartford Courant, Chicago Sun-Times, Milwaukee Journal, St. Louis Post-Dispatch, Louisville Courier-Journal, Washington Post.

Attacking the Court: New York Journal (all Hearst papers), New York News, Baltimore Sun, Boston Globe, Chicago Tribune, Kansas City Star, Los Angeles Times, San Francisco News-Call Bulletin, Washington Star.

in most vehement terms.[3] Most of the Jewish clergy approved the decision.[4] The Protestant ministry was in greater conflict.[5]

The politicians were politicians; most of them who spoke to the question seemed to see an opportunity to make political capital by coming out in favor of God. Congressman Andrews was typical of the southern reaction: "They put the Negroes in to the schools and now they have driven God out of them." Congressman Rooney of New York, a leader in the fight to secure public money for Catholic schools, labeled the decision "asinine," and, with others, saw it as communistic in substance if not in inspiration. Former Presidents Hoover and Eisenhower both were shocked by

[3] Cardinal Spellman's statement was not untypical: "I am shocked and frightened that the Supreme Court has declared unconstitutional a simple and voluntary declaration of belief in God by public school children. The decision strikes at the very heart of the Godly tradition in which America's children have for so long been raised." The Brooklyn *Tablet* labeled the decision "preposterous." The *Catholic News*, the archdiocesan paper for New York, found the "implications . . . appalling." The Jesuit weekly *America* used the adjectives: "asinine," "stupid," "doctrinaire," and "unrealistic." The Catholic spokesmen frequently spoke, nonetheless, of the profit that might be garnered by utilizing the opinion to prove the need for parochial schools to be supported by public funds.

The Vatican also contributed its views, if somewhat belatedly. *Osservatore Romano* expressed doubts about the opinion but, becomingly, in more moderate tones. It stated "regrets" at the "disconcerting" action of the Justices "whatever [their] motivation." *La Civilta Catolica* said: "The possible implications are such as to give rise to certain preoccupations."

[4] The rabbinate was not as unanimous as the Catholic clergy. Most were in accord with the declarations of praise from the New York Board of Rabbis, the Rabbinical Assembly of America, and the Commission of Social Action of Reform Judaism. But there were voices, like that of a Rabbi Kelman of Brooklyn, asserting that: "It is regrettable from the point of view of Judaism that this prayer was banned."

[5] The Reverend Billy Graham thundered, paralogically, against the decision: "God pity our country when we can no longer appeal to God for help." And James A. Pike, Episcopal Bishop of San Francisco, announced that "the Supreme Court has just deconsecrated the nation." More common among those who spoke out for Protestantism was the attitude of Harold E. Fey, editor of the *Christian Century*, and a distinguished group of theologians who joined him: "The Court's decision protects the integrity of the religious conscience and the proper function of religious and governmental institutions."

144   Philip B. Kurland

the Court's action. President Kennedy and Governor Rockefeller—
neither of whom seemed to have any liking for the result—were
outstanding for their moderate reaction. The latter was alone
among all the governors of the United States in opposing a resolution calling for a constitutional amendment to reverse the judgment:

Until the whole question can be considered in terms of the fundamental precept of freedom of religion, which was the basis for the
constitutional provision upon which the Supreme Court based its
opinion, I shall abstain from the endorsement of any hasty action
by the Governors relating to amendment of the Constitution of the
United States.[6]

President Kennedy's statement came in response to a question at
his regular press conference:

The Supreme Court has made its judgment. A good many people
obviously will disagree with it; others will agree with it. But I think
it is important for us, if we're going to maintain our constitutional
principle, that we support Supreme Court decisions even when we
may not agree with them. . . . I would hope that [the people] . . . .
will support the Constitution and the responsibility of the Supreme
Court in interpreting it, which is theirs and given to them by the
. . . Constitution.[7]

"We start down a rough road," said Mr. Justice Jackson in his
dissent in *Zorach,* "when we begin to mix compulsory public education with compulsory godliness."[8] The road was not made any
smoother by the Court's original journey over it, as the immediate
reaction to *Engel* so readily demonstrated. The vituperative assault
following the Regents'-prayer case was not unlike the attack on
the Court when it condemned Illinois' released-time program.[9] The

6 N.Y. Times, July 4, 1962, p. 8, col. 4.

7 N.Y. Times, June 26, 1962, p. 12, col. 1.

8 Zorach v. Clauson, 343 U.S. 306, 325 (1952).

9 McCollum v. Board of Education, 333 U.S. 203 (1948). See KURLAND, RE-
LIGION AND THE LAW 86–90 (1962) (hereinafter RELIGION).
See, *e.g.,* Statement by Catholic Bishops Attacking Secularism as an Evil,
N.Y. Times, Nov. 21, 1948, § 1, p. 63, col. 1; O'NEILL, RELIGION AND EDUCA-
TION UNDER THE CONSTITUTION 219–53, 254–72 (1949).

success of these storm tactics is attested by the Court's retreat in *Zorach*, where Mr. Justice Douglas, writing for the Court, sustained the New York released-time program, distinguishing *McCollum* on gossamer-thin grounds. The Court did not prove so timid about its ruling on public school prayers. On June 17, 1963, it closed its 1962 Term with declarations that the required reading of verses from the Bible and the Lord's Prayer as specified in the statutes of Pennsylvania and Maryland was equally repugnant to the Constitution.[10]

The reaction, if not quite so vituperative, was no less immediate. Nor did there seem to be any change in the positions asserted by the various groups of interested parties. The *New York Times* defended the Court, and the *Chicago Tribune* damned it.[11] The highest representatives of the Catholic Church in the United States, who were in Rome to elect a new Pope, condemned the rulings of the Court in no uncertain terms,[12] although it was obvious that they had had no opportunity to read the opinions rendered by the Court. Senator Ellender, an expert on the subject, referred to the eight-man majority as "eight silly old men."[13] And Senator Strom Thurmond declared: "This constitutes another major triumph for the forces of secularism and atheism which are bent on throwing God completely out of our national life."[14] The John Birch Society again demanded the impeachment of the Chief Justice.[15] Again the Protestant churches were divided,[16] but most spokesmen

[10] School District of Abington v. Schempp, 83 Sup. Ct. 1560 (1963).

[11] *Freedom of Religion*, N.Y. Times, June 19, 1963, p. 32, col. 2; *School Prayer Is Out*, Chicago Tribune, June 18, 1963, p. 18, col. 1. The other newspapers seem to have adhered to earlier positions, except that the New York Herald Tribune expressed the pious hope that some school prayers might be saved. *Let's Not Ban All School Prayers*, N.Y. Herald Tribune, June 18, 1963, p. 18, col. 1.

[12] *3 U.S. Cardinals Decry High Court Prayer Ruling*, N.Y. Times, June 19, 1963, p. 18, col. 1.

[13] N.Y. Herald Tribune, June 19, 1963, p. 8, col. 4.

[14] N.Y. Herald Tribune, June 18, 1963, p. 3, col. 2.

[15] *Id.* at p. 4, col. 5.

[16] Dugan, *Churches Divided, with Most in Favor*, N.Y. Times, June 18, 1963, p. 1, col. 7. Division within various Protestant denominations was not

seemed to support the Court. The Jewish clergy spoke out almost unanimously in favor of the result. In general, the newspapers concluded that the country had accepted the ruling calmly.[17] There is no way of knowing whether this acceptance was due to attempts by various religious and lay leaders to anticipate the decision and prepare their followers for the Court's adherence to precedents[18] or a result of the Court's pronouncement coming in the midst of public preoccupation with violent Negro efforts to secure their constitutional rights—and more.

We do know, however, that the reaction was an unenlightened one in the sense that the spokesmen for the various groups in the community committed themselves without reading and weighing what the Court said. They were all prepared to speak out on the basis of fragmentary news stories and statements of the Court's conclusions. The primary purpose of this essay, therefore, is to set out in some detail the facts on which the Court based its decisions and to reveal the reasons that the Court gave for its conclusions.

---

uncommon. For example, the presiding bishop of the Episcopal Church, The Right Reverend Arthur Lichtenberger, said: "It should be understood that the Court's action is not hostile to religion. These decisions reflect the Court's sense of responsibility to assure freedom and equality to all groups of believers and non-believers. . . ." N.Y. Herald Tribune, June 18, 1963, p. 1, col. 8. However, the most vocal bishop of that same church, the Right Reverend James A. Pike, asserted that the Court had imposed secularism on the public school system. *Id.* at p. 2, col. 3. The Reverend Dr. Billy Graham also repeated his earlier position, this time from Stuttgart, Germany. Once again he was "shocked." *Ibid.*

[17] *Country Calm on Bible Ruling*, N.Y. Herald Tribune, June 19, 1963, p. 8, col. 2. "There were many persons of all faiths, however, who took a 'so what?' attitude. Their view was summed up in the words: 'I couldn't care less.' " N.Y. Times, June 18, 1963, p. 1, col. 7.

[18] See, *e.g.*, Sissel, *Behind the Fight against School Prayer*, Look Magazine, June 18, 1963, p. 25; Katz, *Religion in the Public Schools*, Chicago Sun-Times, June 16, 1963, § 2, p. 1, col. 1. The Reverend H. B. Sissel is Secretary for National Affairs, United Presbyterian Church in the U.S.A. His article was written and published earlier than the date of the magazine would indicate. In addition to being one of the foremost legal authorities on the subject, Professor Katz is chairman of the Protestant Episcopal Church National Church-State Relations Commission.

Only with this information can any evaluation of the Court's actions be meaningful.

I. THE FACTS

The judicial function is exercised within peculiar bounds. Despite the treatment given Supreme Court opinions, even by some of its Justices at times, the fact of the matter is that the Court is a judicial body. Its obligation is to resolve particular controversies between or among parties with real and direct interests. It does not decide abstract questions; it resolves real issues, issues that are based on particular facts elucidated by the trial courts. It is not irrelevant, therefore, to set out the facts of the three cases that gave rise to the two sets of high court opinions with which this essay is concerned.

A. ENGEL V. VITALE

In 1951, the New York Board of Regents became

aware of the dire need, in these days of concentrated attacks by an atheistic way of life upon our world and in these times of rising juvenile delinquency, of crime increasing both numerically and in gravity of offense, with an ever-swelling number of criminals being counted in the younger age groups, of finding ways to pass on America's Moral and Spiritual Heritage to our youth through the public school system.[19]

Among the antidotes to the deterioration of "our youth"—and, presumably, as its contribution to the success of the United States' effort in the cold war—the Board composed a prayer to be utilized at the opening of classes each day in conjunction with the salute to the flag. The prayer: "Almighty God, we acknowledge our dependence upon Thee, and we beg Thy blessings upon us, our parents, our teachers and our country."

However one may evaluate other contested facts in the record, it is quite clear that the intention of the Board in recommending

---

[19] Brief for the Board of Regents of the University of the State of New York as Amicus Curiae, p. 14, Engel v. Vitale, 370 U.S. 421 (1962). (Capitalization in original.)

the use of this prayer was to inculcate in the school children "the belief in a Supreme Being."[20] At the same time, in achieving this goal, the Board wished to avoid giving offense to any of the country's three major religious faiths: Protestant, Catholic, Jewish. To avoid infringing on the rights of any who might not accept the orthodoxy of any of these religions, the Board provided for voluntary abstention from participation for those who chose not to number themselves among "all men and women of good will" who would "subscribe" to the Board's "program."[21]

In July of 1958, the Board of Education for a school district in New Hyde Park, New York, provided by resolution that the Regents' prayer be utilized in its schools. It ordered the district principal to see "that this be instituted as a daily procedure to follow the Salute to the flag."[22] Accordingly, the practice was adopted in New Hyde Park schools. The prayer was said aloud at the beginning of classes each day, led by the teacher or a student singled out by the teacher for this purpose.[23] Possibly before,[24] but certainly after, the order of the trial court in this litigation,[25] teachers were instructed to abstain from encouraging participation by unwilling children, who were to be excused from participation or permitted to absent themselves from the classrooms on written requests of their parents or guardians.

In January, 1959, five parents of children attending schools in New Hyde Park, all citizens of the United States and of New York, all taxpayers of the school district,[26] removed themselves from the Regents' category of "men and women of good will" by seeking an order in the nature of mandamus from the trial court of general jurisdiction to compel the discontinuance of the Regents'-prayer ceremony in the schools of the district. The objections asserted were that

the saying of the said prayer and the manner and setting in which it is said violate the prohibition against laws respecting an estab-

---

[20] Record, pp. 28–29.
[21] 370 U.S. at 423.
[22] Record, p. 40.
[23] *Id.* at 14, 24–27, 66.

[24] *Id.* at 27, 66.
[25] *Id.* at 170–73.
[26] *Id.* at 11–12.

lishment of religion [and] . . . laws prohibiting the free exercise of religion. . . .[27]

Justice Meyer of the Supreme Court of Nassau County wrote an exhaustive and erudite opinion[28] in which he ordered the Board of Education to issue regulations clarifying the rights of students to abstain from participation but ruled that, with this safeguard, there was no violation of either the separation or the freedom clause of the First Amendment. The Supreme Court opinion on which he rested most heavily was *Zorach v. Clauson*.[29] The Appellate Division affirmed per curiam, but Mr. Justice Beldock added his approval on the ground that "the prayer here involved *does not constitute religious teaching*."[30] The Court of Appeals divided.[31] The majority found no infringement of religious freedom because of the right of the pupils to abstain from participation. It found no establishment barrier because:

Belief in a Supreme Being is as essential and permanent a feature of the American governmental system as is freedom of worship, equality under the law and due process of law. Like them it is an American absolute, an application of the natural law beliefs on which the Re-

---

[27] *Id*. at 16. More specifically, they asserted that the ceremony was unconstitutional because it: (1) "entails the use of the public school system . . . the time and efforts of the teachers and the staff . . ."; (2) "constitute[s] the teaching of religion and religious practices in a form, manner and setting which is contrary to the religion and religious practices of [four of] . . . the petitioners . . . and . . . their children" and others in the district; (3) is "contrary to the beliefs concerning such matters" of the non-religious "petitioner and his children" and others in the district; (4) has "necessarily resulted in the exercise of coercion upon the children . . . to engage, against their will, in the saying of a religious prayer . . ."; (5) is "sectarian and denominational" and "favor[s] one or more religions and religious practices over others"; (6) "favor[s] the belief in religion over non-belief therein"; and (7) has "necessarily resulted in divisiveness among the students . . . and among their parents. . . ." *Id*. at 15–16.

[28] 18 N.Y. Misc.2d 659, 191 N.Y.S.2d 453 (Sup. Ct. Nass. Co. 1959).

[29] 343 U.S. 306 (1952). See RELIGION, 86–90.

[30] 11 N.Y. App. Div.2d 340, 343, 206 N.Y.S.2d 183, 186 (1960). (Emphasis in original.)

[31] 10 N.Y.2d 174, 176 N.E.2d 579, 218 N.Y.S.2d 659 (1961).

public was founded and which in turn presuppose an Omnipotent Being.[32]

Zorach v. Clauson and *Holy Trinity v. United States*[33] were the only Supreme Court decisions which gave aid and comfort to the majority. It was the minority opinion, written by Judge Dye for himself and Judge Fuld, that attempted an analysis of Supreme Court opinions and concluded from them that the Regents'-prayer mandate was unconstitutional.

B. ABINGTON SCHOOL DISTRICT V. SCHEMPP

The Pennsylvania litigation had a long history and, were it not for the fact that the Schempps were blessed with more than one child, the case might have evaporated in the pattern of *Doremus v. Board of Education*,[34] in which the case was mooted by the graduation of the school child. Indeed, the oldest of the Schempp children had been graduated from the public high school before the trial court first reached a decision in the case.

At the time the case was first decided, the three-judge trial court, presided over by Chief Judge Biggs of the Court of Appeals for the Third Circuit, determined that the children were in attendance at Abington public schools pursuant to Pennsylvania statute, and that:

In each of said schools attended by the minor plaintiffs there is an opening period each day observed by the reading of ten verses of the Bible.

The reading of the Bible as aforesaid each day is followed by a standing recitation in unison of that portion of the New Testament known as the Lord's Prayer.

The attendance of all students in both of the aforesaid schools at the ceremony of the Bible reading and recitation of the Lord's Prayer is compulsory.

[32] *Id.* at 181–82, 176 N.E.2d at 582, 218 N.Y.S.2d at 662. It might be suggested that at least one difference exists between "natural law beliefs" and "freedom of worship, equality under the law and due process of law." The latter are specified as within the protection of the Constitution; the former are not.

[33] 143 U.S. 457 (1892). See RELIGION, 26–27.

[34] 342 U.S. 429 (1952).

The practice of the daily reading of ten verses of the Bible in the public schools of Abington Township constitutes religious instruction and the promotion of religiousness.

The practice of the daily reading of ten verses of the Bible together with the daily recitation of the Lord's Prayer in the public schools of Abington Township is a religious ceremony.[35]

From these findings, the conclusions of law were ineluctable. The practices in question violated both the free-exercise and establishment clauses of the First Amendment, applied to the states through the Fourteenth. While the case was pending on appeal to the Supreme Court, however, the Pennsylvania legislature amended the statute to provide: "Any child shall be excused from such Bible reading, or attending such Bible reading, upon the written request of his parent or guardian."[36] In light of the amendment, the Supreme Court remanded the case to the trial court for further proceedings.[37] The trial court permitted the amendment of the plaintiffs' pleadings.[38] After rehearing the court amended its findings of fact to reveal that the children were free to abstain from participation in the Bible-reading and amended its conclusion of law to rest the invalidity of the statute solely upon the establishment provision.[39]

The record also revealed that the practice in the Abington Township schools having loud-speaker systems was to broadcast the Bible-reading and prayers throughout the classrooms;[40] that students chosen for the purpose could read any ten verses they preferred; that the only Bible distributed to the teachers for this purpose was the King James version of the Bible; that students ex-

[35] Schempp v. School District of Abington Township, 177 F. Supp. 398, 408 (E.D. Pa. 1959).

[36] PA. STAT. ANN. tit. 24, § 15–1516 (Purdon's 1962).

[37] 364 U.S. 298 (1960).

[38] 195 F. Supp. 518 (E.D. Pa. 1961).

[39] 201 F. Supp. 815, 820 (E.D. Pa. 1962). The decision was rendered on Feb. 1, 1962, some months before the *Engel* case was decided by the Supreme Court.

[40] *Cf.* Public Utilities Commission v. Pollak, 343 U.S. 451 (1952).

cused pursuant to the statute were required to spend the time in the hallways outside their home classrooms while the reading and prayer session was conducted.

In each of its opinions the trial court relied principally upon *McCollum v. Board of Education.*[41]

C. MURRAY V. CURLETT

Like *Engel* and unlike *Schempp, Murray v. Curlett*[42] came to the Supreme Court through a state court system. The facts were essentially the same as in the *Schempp* case, except that the petitioners, mother and son, alleged that they were atheists. In Baltimore, as in Pennsylvania, as a result of the action taken by petitioners the governing rule was amended to provide that students may be excused from opening exercises that consisted of reading from the Bible and reciting the Lord's Prayer.

The Maryland Court of Appeals divided four to three on the question, stated by the majority thus: "whether the daily opening exercises of the Baltimore City public schools—wherein the Holy Bible is read and the Lord's Prayer is recited—violate the constitutional rights of a student and his mother who claim they are atheists."[43] The majority answered the question in the negative, relying principally on *Zorach* and on cases decided by other state courts, including *Engel v. Vitale.* The more persuasive minority opinion by Chief Judge Brune reached the opposite conclusion on a reading of *Everson, McCollum,* and *Torcaso v. Watkins.*[44] With some prescience, Chief Judge Brune anticipated that the decision in *Engel,* which was then pending in the Supreme Court, "will be determinative of this [case]."[45]

[41] 333 U.S. 203 (1948).

[42] 228 Md. 239, 179 A.2d 698 (1962).

[43] *Id.* at 241, 179 A.2d at 699.

[44] 367 U.S. 488 (1961). See RELIGION, 107–8. It was the Maryland Court of Appeals that was reversed in that case, too.

[45] 228 Md. at 261, 179 A.2d at 710.

II. The Supreme Court's Opinions

A. ENGEL V. VITALE

By the time the *Engel* case was presented to the Supreme Court for decision, the arguments had been reduced to a small number, and the issues were posed in extremely general terms. Although the petition for certiorari had kept open the possibility of urging violation of the freedom clause in accordance with the position taken by the dissenters in the Court of Appeals, by the time the brief on the merits was presented, only the establishment issue was argued.[46] The primary authority relied upon by the petitioners was *McCollum*. The respondents rested largely on the long-continued existence of the practice of prayer in public places and on *Zorach*. Under the circumstances one might have anticipated that the Court would be required, at least, to reconcile the *McCollum* and *Zorach* cases. But the Court's opinions were as broad and general as the arguments and the opinions in the lower courts. The only thing left clear by the opinions was that, if the decisions of the past had failed to produce a governing principle, no remedy of that defect was to be found in *Engel*.

Mr. Justice Black's opinion for the Court was joined by the Chief Justice, and Justices Clark, Harlan, and Brennan. Mr. Justice Douglas wrote a concurring opinion, and Mr. Justice Stewart wrote a dissent. The reader gets an impression of the Justices of the majority walking on eggs and of the two minority Justices stamping after them.

The majority reached its conclusion without the citation of a single prior Supreme Court decision, except for a reference to the history of the First Amendment contained in *Everson*.[47] History purported to be the main reliance of the Court. Black started with the proposition that the ceremony commanded by the Board of Education was a religious one:

[46] Petition for Certiorari, p. 4; Brief for Petitioners, p. 3, Engel v. Vitale, 370 U.S. 421 (1962).

[47] 370 U.S. at 428–29, n.11.

There can, of course, be no doubt that New York's program of daily classroom invocation of God's blessings as prescribed in the Regents' prayer is a religious activity. It is a solemn avowal of divine faith and supplication for the blessings of the Almighty.[48]

He relied on a recitation of history to show that once government enters the business of prescribing prayers it invites the exercise of pressures from various groups within the community as to the content of such prayers. This kind of activity has been proved by history to be destructive of the public peace. And, like Father John Courtney Murray,[49] Black thought that the First Amendment was framed for the preservation of the public peace by the avoidance of such contests. To prevent this evil, the Constitution forbade the coincidence of governmental and religious authority.

By the time of the adoption of the Constitution, our history shows that there was a widespread awareness among many Americans of the dangers of a union of Church and State. . . . The First Amendment was added to the Constitution to stand as a guarantee that neither the power nor the prestige of the Federal Government would be used to control, support or influence the kinds of prayer the American people can say—that the people's religions must not be subjected to the pressures of government for change each time a new political administration is elected to office.[50]

The Court rejected the notion that the absence of "compulsion" eliminated the problem:

The Establishment Clause, unlike the Free Exercise Clause, does not depend upon any showing of direct governmental compulsion and is violated by the enactment of laws which establish an official religion whether those laws operate directly to coerce nonobserving individuals or not. This is not to say, of course, that laws officially prescribing a particular form of religious worship do not involve coercion of such individuals. When the power, prestige and financial support of government is placed behind a particular religious belief, the indirect coercive pressure upon religious minorities to conform to the prevailing officially approved religion is plain. But the purposes underlying the Establishment Clause go much further than that. Its first

[48] *Id.* at 424.

[49] Murray, We Hold These Truths (1960).

[50] 370 U.S. at 429–30.

and most immediate purpose rested on the belief that a union of government and religion tends to destroy government and to degrade religion. . . . The Establishment Clause thus stands as an expression of principle on the part of the Founders of our Constitution that religion is too personal, too sacred, too holy, to permit its "unhallowed perversion" by a civil magistrate.[51]

The Court also rejected the proposition that this required separation of church and state exhibited a hostility to religion:

It has been argued that to apply the Constitution in such a way as to prohibit state laws respecting an establishment of religious services in public schools is to indicate a hostility toward religion or toward prayer. Nothing, of course, could be more wrong. . . . [The authors of the Bill of Rights] knew that the First Amendment, which tried to put an end to governmental control of religion and of prayer, was not written to destroy either. . . . It is neither sacrilegious nor antireligious to say that each separate government in this country should stay out of the business of writing or sanctioning official prayers and leave that purely religious function to the people themselves and to those the people choose to look to for religious guidance.[52]

The *de minimus* notion was similarly treated by reference to Madison's *Memorial and Remonstrance against Religious Assessments*.[53] And the parade of horribles that suggested that the use of the word "God" in public activities was within the ban stated in the opinion was disposed of by a footnote: "Such patriotic or ceremonial occasions bear no true resemblance to the unquestioned religious exercise that the State of New York has sponsored in this instance."[54]

The majority opinion thus dealt with every argument raised by respondents or by the courts below in support of the Regents' prayer ceremony except that which rested on *Zorach*. As to the relevance or vitality of that case, the Court was completely silent.

The holding of the Court was, indeed, a narrow one:

[T]he constitutional prohibition against laws respecting an establishment of religion must at least mean that in this country it is no part

[51] *Id.* at 430–32.   [53] *Id.* at 436.

[52] *Id.* at 433–35.   [54] *Id.* at 435, n.21.

of the business of government to compose official prayers for any group of the American people to recite as a part of a religious program carried on by government.[55]

It was the concurring and dissenting opinions that read into the Court's judgment a breadth and effect that the Court specifically disavowed. And it was this reading that was accepted by the divines as an appropriate target for criticism.[56]

Mr. Justice Douglas' concurring opinion gave new meaning to the proposition: "Millions for defense but not one cent for tribute." As he not infrequently does in other complex cases, he found the problem simple of statement and equally simple of solution: "The point for decision is whether the Government can constitutionally finance a religious exercise. Our system at the federal and state levels is presently honeycombed with such financing."[57] Unlike Black, he found "no element of compulsion or coercion in New York's regulation. . . ."[58] This was consistent with the opinion he wrote for the Court in *Zorach*, but *Zorach* was not used to bolster this conclusion. Nor was it distinguished in any way. *Zorach* was cited only for its famed, troublemaking, and essentially meaningless statement: "We are a religious people whose institutions presuppose a Supreme Being."[59] He did distinguish *Mc-Collum* on this score. For in that case "the influence of the teaching staff was . . . brought to bear on the student body, to support the instilling of religious principles."[60] Indeed, the only case that he thought to stand in the way of his conclusion was *Everson*, "which allowed taxpayers' money to be used to pay 'the bus fares of parochial school pupils as a part of a general program under which' the fares of pupils attending public and other schools were also paid."[61] This statement of the facts of *Everson* is erroneous, for there was no such "general program" involved in *Everson*,[62] but the error is unimportant to Douglas' thesis. The appropriate

[55] *Id*. at 425.

[56] See text at notes 3–5 *supra*.

[57] 370 U.S. at 437.

[58] *Id*. at 438.

[59] 343 U.S. at 313, quoted 370 U.S. at 442.

[60] 370 U.S. at 439.

[61] *Id*. at 443.

[62] See RELIGION, 80–85.

principle that he stated in a footnote is not inconsistent with anything that Black said. "The First Amendment . . . . prevented secular sanction to any religious ceremony, dogma, or rite."[63] But the guiding principle of his opinion is both narrower and broader: not one cent of the taxpayers' money may be used for or given to any activity or institution connected with religion. This comes closer to non-judicial statements by Douglas than to any principle or judgment enunciated by the Court, except that in the dissenting opinion of Mr. Justice Rutledge in the *Everson* case which Douglas quoted in his *Engel* opinion.[64] Douglas, like some of the Court's critics, would seem to have been more concerned with the problem of federal aid to parochial education than with the facts of the case immediately before him. His extra-judicial conclusion, stated in terms not dissimilar to his language in *Engel,* was that any such aid would be unconstitutional.[65]

Mr. Justice Stewart's dissent rested on the proposition that the Court's judgment infringed the rights of the majority: "to deny the wish of these school children to join in reciting this prayer is to deny them the opportunity of sharing in the spiritual heritage of our Nation."[66] He thus attributed to the Court the decision of a much harder case than that with which it was presented. His proposition assumed that the prayer ceremony was initiated by the children or their parents rather than being imposed by the Board of Education.[67] In any event, reading the opinion of the Court as broadly as did Douglas, Stewart found it inconsistent with the

[63] 370 U.S. at 442, n.7.

[64] *Id.* at 443–44. It is interesting to note that Douglas found this proposition unconvincing in *Everson,* in which he was a crucial member of the majority.

[65] See HUTCHINS, TWO FACES OF FEDERALISM 58–60 (1961).

[66] 370 U.S. at 445.

[67] The distinction was recognized even by the New York American Legion. At its 1962 State convention, it passed a resolution stating: "It is manifestly clear that a prayer chosen by the pupils or their parents and voluntarily recited by them at the beginning of each school day is not a procedure coming within the prohibition of [the Court's] decision or the First Amendment to the Constitution." Certainly it is not "manifestly clear." But it presents a different problem from that resolved by the Court in *Engel.*

quotation from *Zorach*, which means all things to all men, and to Stewart a justification for state-sponsored religious ceremonies.

B. SCHEMPP AND MURRAY

Whether because of the uproar that followed the *Engel* case, as suggested by Anthony Lewis,[68] or because of a recognition that the issues deserve more explication than *Engel* afforded, the *Schempp*[69] decision called forth five different opinions and more than one hundred pages of explanation. It might have been the better part of wisdom had the Court taken the hint given by Chief Judge Brune and simply affirmed *Schempp* and reversed *Murray* per curiam on the authority of *Engel*. Certainly the Court did not, by its opinions, avoid the criticism that was necessarily forthcoming. Critics of this sort, as the Court well knows, don't read the opinions. Nor, unfortunately, do the opinions in *Schempp* spread light where *Engel* had left only darkness. The opinions do reveal a groping for doctrine that should be applied, but it cannot be said that the search has been crowned with success.

1. *The Court's opinion.*—The opinion of the Court was written by Mr. Justice Clark, and all the other members of the Court concurred, except Mr. Justice Stewart, who adhered to the position he took in *Engel*. After stating the facts, Mr. Justice Clark paid homage to the proposition that religion is an integral part of American life and history: Not only are we a church-affiliated people, but the Founders were believers in God; moreover, the Congress and the Court open their sessions with prayer, and our armed forces and other public agencies maintain chaplains. But, Mr. Justice Clark added, we are also a people devoted to religious freedom.

---

[68] Lewis, *Public Mood Plays Big Role in Court Rulings*, N.Y. Times, June 23, 1963, § 4, p. 4, col. 1: "Few cases in recent years have produced so emotional a reaction from the public as did the Regents' prayer decision last year, or such violent attacks on the Justices. The Court, for its part, has seldom shown awareness of public opinion more plainly than in its handling of the new prayer cases that came down this week."

[69] Hereafter both *Schempp* and *Murray* will generally be referred to collectively as *Schempp*.

The Justice then announced the notion of "neutrality" that he derived from "Judge Alphonzo Taft, father of the revered Chief Justice,"[70] who stated in an unpublished opinion: "The government is neutral, and, while protecting all [religions], it prefers none, and it disparages none."[71] But, before applying this general proposition to the facts before the Court, Clark undertook to restate two principles that the Court had announced in past decisions. First, he said, the Court has clearly accepted the proposition that the religion clauses of the First Amendment are applicable to the states through the Fourteenth.[72] Second, it is clear that the Court has rejected the notion that the establishment clause forbids only the preference of one religion over another.[73] In emphasizing these points he was obviously directing himself to outside critics, for no party to these cases put these propositions in issue.

The opinion takes a peculiar turn at this point. Part IV consists of quotations from several Supreme Court decisions presumably touching on "the interrelationship of the Establishment and Free Exercise Clauses. . . ."[74] The quotations are from *Cantwell*,[75] *Everson*,[76] *McCollum*,[77] *Zorach*,[78] *McGowan*,[79] *Torcaso*,[80] and *Engel*.[81] The facts of the cases are ignored, perhaps to the end that their holdings need not be reconciled. The language quoted supports the proposition that the Court adheres to a notion of separation of church and state; it does not indicate the proper relationship between the two clauses. The conclusion would seem to be

[70] 83 Sup. Ct. at 1567.

[71] *Ibid.*

[72] *Id.* at 1567–68.

[73] *Id.* at 1568–69.

[74] *Id.* at 1569.

[75] Cantwell v. Connecticut, 310 U.S. 296 (1940). See RELIGION, 51–54.

[76] Everson v. Board of Education, 330 U.S. 1 (1947). See RELIGION, 80–85.

[77] McCollum v. Board of Education, 333 U.S. 203 (1948).

[78] Zorach v. Clauson, 343 U.S. 306 (1952).

[79] McGowan v. Maryland, 366 U.S. 420 (1961). See RELIGION, 97–106.

[80] Torcaso v. Watkins, 367 U.S. 488 (1961).

[81] Engel v. Vitale, 370 U.S. 421 (1962). See Kurland, *The Regents' Prayer Case: "Full of Sound and Fury, Signifying . . ."* [1962] SUP. CT. REV. 1.

that both clauses point to a principle of neutrality; in this regard, they "may overlap."[82]

The opinion next sets forth the standard appropriate to the
establishment clause:

The test may be stated as follows: what are the purpose and the primary effect of the enactment? If either is the advancement or inhibition
[sic] of religion then the enactment exceeds the scope of legislative
power as circumscribed by the Constitution. That is to say that to
withstand the strictures of the Establishment Clause there must be
a secular legislative purpose and a primary effect that neither ad-
vances nor inhibits religion.[83]

This assertion necessarily raises the question: If the establishment
clause is concerned with protecting against both "advancement"
and "inhibition" of religion, what is the function of the free-
exercise clause? For it is clear, in the opinions of the Court, that
the two, although overlapping, serve distinct functions. Unfortunately, Mr. Justice Clark's answer is confusing:

The Free Exercise Clause, likewise considered many times here, with-
draws from legislative power, state and federal, the exertion of any
restraint on the free exercise of religion. Its purpose is to secure
religious liberty in the individual by prohibiting any invasions thereof
by civil authority. Hence it is necessary in a free exercise case for
one to show the coercive effect of the enactment as it operates against
him in the practice of his religion. The distinction between the two
clauses is apparent—a violation of the Free Exercise Clause is predi-

[82] 83 Sup. Ct. at 1571.

[83] *Ibid. Cf.* RELIGION, 17–18: "The utilization or application of these
clauses in conjunction is difficult. For if the command is that inhibitions not be
placed by the state on religious activity, it is equally forbidden the state to
confer favors upon religious activity. These commands would be impossible
of effectuation unless they are read together as creating a doctrine more akin
to the reading of the equal protection clause than to the due process clause,
i.e., they must be read to mean that religion may not be used as a basis for
classification for purposes of governmental action, whether that action be the
conferring of rights or privileges or the imposition of duties or obligations. . . .
"[T]he thesis proposed here as the proper construction of the religion clauses
of the first amendment is that the freedom and separation clauses should be
read as a single precept that government cannot utilize religion as a standard
for action or inaction because these clauses prohibit classification in terms of
religion either to confer a benefit or to impose a burden." Also see *id.* at 112.

cated on coercion while the Establishment Clause violation need not be so attended.[84]

Having come close to announcing the purpose of the establishment clause to be the same that *Religion and the Law* finds in both clauses read together,[85] Clark then confounded the matter by speaking of the free-exercise clause as accomplishing the same end in a different manner. Apparently only the establishment clause precludes the "advancement of religion." But both clauses, according to Mr. Justice Clark, prohibit inhibition of religious activity: The free-exercise clause prohibits it by precluding the use of coercion; the establishment clause, by restricting some undefined non-coercive methods.[86]

From this point on, however, the opinion has clear sailing. The recitation of the Lord's Prayer and Bible-reading are religious exercises sponsored by the state and, under the principle announced, are necessarily violative of the establishment clause. *Zorach* is distinguished:

These exercises are prescribed as part of the curricular activities of students who are required by law to attend school. They are held in the school buildings under the supervision and with the participation of teachers employed in those schools. None of these factors, other than compulsory school attendance, was present in the program upheld in Zorach v. Clauson.[87]

Never mind that *Zorach* does not conform to the announced principle. (For clearly the "purpose and primary effect" of the released-time legislation approved in *Zorach* "is the advancement . . . of religion.") That case remains, at least in form, to confound the bench and bar, although it may shortly be, or may now have been, distinguished to death.

The Court properly and quickly disposed of the arguments that the functions of the prayers and readings are really secular.[88] Moreover, "it is no defense to urge that the religious practices

---

[84] 83 Sup. Ct. at 1572.

[85] See note 83 *supra*.

[86] 83 Sup. Ct. at 1571–72.

[87] *Id.* at 1572.

[88] *Ibid.*

here may be relatively minor encroachments on the First Amendment."[89]

The argument that failure to support religious exercises in the schools is the equivalent of joining the power of government to the forces of secularism (essentially Mr. Justice Stewart's argument here and in *Engel*) was specifically rejected:

We agree of course that the State may not establish a "religion of secularism" in the sense of affirmatively opposing or showing hostility to religion, thus "preferring those who believe in no religion over those who do believe." Zorach v. Clauson, supra, 343 U.S. at 314. We do not agree, however, that this decision in any sense has that effect.[90]

The Court also disposed of the bogeyman that the schools may no longer study the Bible or religion, for what it condemns are "religious exercises"[91] not intellectual appraisals.

The problem of standing was inadequately disposed of in a footnote.[92] And in another footnote the Court left open the question of supplying chaplains for the military.[93]

The conclusion of the Court's opinion is touching, if not enlightening:

The place of religion in our society is an exalted one, achieved through a long tradition of reliance on the home, the church and the inviolable citadel of the individual heart and mind. We have come to recognize through bitter experience that it is not within the power of government to invade that citadel, whether its purpose or effect be to aid or oppose, to advance or retard. In the relationship between man and religion, the State is firmly committed to a position of neutrality. Though the application of that rule requires interpretation of a delicate sort, the rule itself is clearly and concisely stated in the words of the First Amendment.[94]

However cryptic the message contained in this peroration, the Court's opinion might have been a long step toward the development of a governing principle in the application of the religion clauses of the First Amendment if no more had been said. Unfor-

[89] *Id.* at 1573.   [90] *Ibid.*   [91] *Ibid.*

[92] *Id.* at 1572–73, n.9. See text following note 136 *infra.*

[93] *Id.* at 1573, n.10.   [94] *Id.* at 1574.

tunately, the twenty-three pages contributed by Mr. Justice Clark were but a small part of the Justices' expressions on the subject. And it should be kept in mind that only the Chief Justice, Mr. Justice Black, and Mr. Justice White—not a majority—were content to rest on this opinion alone.

2. *Mr. Justice Brennan's opinion.*—The twenty-three pages written by Mr. Justice Clark were not only dwarfed but obscured by the seventy-seven pages it took Mr. Justice Brennan to express how and why he joined "fully in the opinion and judgment of the Court."[95] For it is quite clear that the force and effect of the statement of concurrence in the Court's opinion is diluted, if not destroyed, by the fact that Mr. Justice Brennan's thesis is quite different from, indeed contradictory of, that put forth by Mr. Justice Clark.

At the outset of his opinion, Mr. Justice Brennan revealed his own understanding of the problem and the answer that is provided by the First Amendment. It is an answer that also speaks in terms of neutrality, but with a difference:

The fact is that the line which separates the secular from the sectarian in American life is elusive. The difficulty of defining the boundary with precision inheres in a paradox central to our scheme of liberty. While our institutions reflect a firm conviction that we are a religious people, those institutions by solemn constitutional injunction may not officially involve religion in such a way as to prefer, discriminate against, or oppress, a particular sect or religion. Equally the Constitution enjoins those involvements of religious with secular institutions which (a) serve the essentially religious activities of religious institutions; (b) employ the organs of government for essentially religious purposes; or (c) use essentially religious means to serve governmental ends where secular means would suffice.[96]

It is clear from this central refrain of Mr. Justice Brennan that he had his eye on many problems other than praying and Bible-reading in public schools. Certainly there are some negative pregnants in his theme. Among them are the propositions that those activities of religious institutions that are not "essentially religious" do not fall under constitutional condemnation and, what is more, even

[95] *Id.* at 1576.   [96] *Ibid.*

essentially religious means may be used to serve governmental ends where secular means would not suffice.

Despite the lengthy opinion on which he then embarked, Mr. Justice Brennan first recognized that the decision in *Engel* sufficed to decide the cases immediately before the Court:

The reasons we gave only last Term . . . for finding in the New York Regents' prayer an impermissible establishment of religion, compel the same judgment of the practices at bar. . . . [I]t is constitutionally irrelevant that the State has not composed the material for the inspirational exercises presently involved.[97]

After an introduction that disposed of essentials he turned first to the lesson of history. He used history not to determine past practices but to discover the objective to be achieved by the First Amendment: the avoidance of "those official involvements of religion which would tend to foster or discourage religious worship or belief."[98] He made four points in his consideration of the relevance of history. First, that "the historical record is at best ambiguous. . . ."[99] Second, that circumstances have changed so vastly that general education, once the function of the church, has long since become the function of the state, making earlier practices irrelevant to current conditions. Third, that circumstances have changed, not only with reference to educational facilities, but also by reason of the fact that "our religious composition makes us a vastly more diverse people than were our forefathers."[100] The fourth point is somewhat elusive: The public schools afford a peculiar function, "a uniquely *public* function: the training of American citizens in an atmosphere free of parochial, divisive, or separatist influences of any sort—an atmosphere in which children may assimilate a heritage common to all American groups and religions."[101] The difficult point comes in his proposition that it is constitutionally necessary to preserve the choice between such schools and such education, on the one hand, and sectarian educa-

[97] *Ibid.*

[98] *Id.* at 1578.

[99] *Id.* at 1579.

[100] *Id.* at 1581.

[101] *Id.* at 1582. (Emphasis in original.)

tion, on the other. In short, a reaffirmation of *Pierce v. Society of Sisters*,[102] but from another direction.

The second section of the Brennan opinion tendered three more lessons. One: courts may not decide theological questions. Two: *Everson* was the Court's first decision of a question under the establishment clause. Three: the free-exercise clause is relevant to the resolution of establishment clause questions. For Mr. Justice Brennan this meant a survey of the Court's opinions on the subject beginning with *Reynolds*.[103]

Contained in this section is one important proposition that may prove fruitful in future cases. It is the suggestion that the difference between *Barnette* and *Hamilton*[104] lay in the difference between the ages of the parties involved. The state, he suggests, has more leeway in dealing with adults than it does when dealing with children.[105] The importance, of course, may be found in matters involving aid to colleges as distinguished from grade schools, in the provision of military chaplains, or, indeed, in the prescription of prayer with an allowance for voluntary abstention when the schools controlled or the audiences involved are mature, at least chronologically.

The third part of Mr. Justice Brennan's opinion deals with the incorporation in the Fourteenth Amendment of the provisions of the religion clauses, which thereby became applicable to the states. His conclusion is that the establishment, no less than the free-exercise, clause has become so incorporated. In the course of dealing with this problem, he, like most courts, lawyers, and students of the problem, felt the necessity for reconciling *McCollum* and

---

102 268 U.S. 510 (1925). See RELIGION, 27–28.

103 Reynolds v. United States, 98 U.S. 145 (1878). Mr. Justice Brennan's frequent references to *Religion and the Law* call for an expression of gratitude for his taking notice of the work. I regret only that it did not lead him to acquiesce in the thesis, see note 83 *supra*, as well as in the statement of the cases.

104 West Virginia State Board of Education v. Barnette, 319 U.S. 624 (1943); Hamilton v. Regents, 293 U.S. 245 (1934). See RELIGION, 38–47.

105 83 Sup. Ct. at 1587.

Zorach. His distinction is no more persuasive than others that have been offered:

The deeper difference was that the McCollum program placed the religious instructor in the public school classroom in precisely the position of authority held by the regular teachers of secular subjects, while the Zorach program did not. . . . [T]he Constitution does not permit that prestige and capacity for influence to be augmented by investiture of all the symbols of authority at the command of the lay teacher for the enhancement of secular instruction.[106]

The section ended with a review of the establishment cases, concluding with the somewhat dubious proposition earlier stated: "But the teaching of both Torcaso and the Sunday Law Cases is that government may not employ religious means to serve secular interests, however legitimate they may be, at least without the clearest demonstration that nonreligious means will not suffice."[107] This proposition has all the makings of a bomb to be set for explosion at some indefinite future time.

The discussion preceding the last portion of the opinion is concerned with the problems immediately before the Court. The standing issue is brushed under the rug by a footnote.[108] The easy proposition is put first. The result in *Schempp* and *Murray* necessarily flows from *Engel.* The opinion then derives support from the minority of state courts that had reached similar conclusions under their own constitutions,[109] with emphasis on *Ring v. Board of Education,*[110] a 1910 Illinois Supreme Court case decided at the behest of Catholic children objecting to the reading of the King James edition of the Bible and the Protestant version of the Lord's Prayer. From the majority of cases that had approved such activities, Brennan derived the conclusion that the courts recognized them as religious in nature, however they ra-

[106] *Id.* at 1592–93.

[107] *Id.* at 1594.

[108] *Id.* at 1594–95, n.30. See text following note 136 *infra.*

[109] *Id.* at 1599–1600.

[110] 245 Ill. 334, 92 N.E. 251 (1910). See text accompanying notes 133–34 *infra.*

tionalized the permission they afforded the school authorities to engage in them. He was unpersuaded by the proposition that these recitations served secular functions, or at least that they served secular functions that could not be accomplished by secular means. For him there was adequate evidence that public prayer was offensive, not only to those who might disagree with the contents of the devotional service, but even to those who adhered to the substance but rejected the method. Moreover, he cast doubt on the efficacy of this Bible-reading and prayer in inculcating religious beliefs. (This did not bring him to the conclusion that the exercises were, therefore, non-religious in nature.) He also rejected the proposition that the exercises might be sustained because they afforded a "common core" theology: "nonsectarian religious practices, equally with sectarian exercises, violate the Establishment Clause."[111] Finally, he held that the provision for exemption from attendance did not afford a basis for sustaining the activities attacked. He rested here on both the proposition that coercion was irrelevant to the establishment clause problem and that, in fact, there was coercion in the circumstances under which children would have to separate themselves from their peers on grounds that would almost necessarily adversely affect their relationships.[112]

The last part of the Justice's opinion is devoted to the parade of imaginary horribles offered the Court by the defenders of the prayer recitals, both within the courtrooms and outside. He recited the various situations in which accommodations had been made between religious practices and governmental functions and appeared to be approving the validity of such activity—whether it was churches and chaplains for military establishments and penal institutions, recital of prayers in legislative assemblies, the study of the Bible and religious literature in schools, tax exemptions to religious organizations, the utilization of religious considerations in "public welfare programs," or governmental activities that were religious in origin but are no longer so considered.[113] These statements reveal a direct conflict between the opinions of Brennan and Douglas.

[111] 83 Sup. Ct. at 1606.   [112] *Id*. at 1606–9.   [113] *Id*. at 1609–14.

Mr. Justice Brennan's opinion is an exhaustive survey of the cases and literature on the subject of the religion clauses of the First Amendment. It would seem to have been written by a judge who will not accept the validity of a precedent unless he has himself examined the subject and concurred in the earlier judgment. By this effort Mr. Justice Brennan has, at least, prepared himself for decision of the cases yet to come in this area. It is doubtful that he has shown the way to others.

3. *Mr. Justice Douglas' opinion.*—It is usually possible to praise Mr. Justice Douglas' opinions for their brevity, if for nothing else. He, too, purported to concur in the opinion of the Court. He, too, would seem to have had many things other than Bible-reading on his mind. His opinion, a repetition of his concurrence in *Engel,* is a declaration that public aid to parochial schools is unconstitutional. In his opinion there are two reasons why the decisions reached in these cases were demanded by the establishment clause. First, the clause prohibits the state's conducting religious ceremonies, and these activities were religious ceremonies. Second—and implicitly more important—the clause forbids the states' contributing any financial resources, however small, to promote religious exercises. The two concluding paragraphs in the opinion are fully expressive of the Justice's attitude:

The most effective way to establish an institution is to finance it; and this truth is reflected in the appeals by church groups for public funds to finance their religious schools. Financing a church either in its strictly religious activities or in its other activities is equally unconstitutional, as I understand the Establishment Clause. Budgets for one activity may be technically separable from budgets for others. But the institution is an inseparable whole, a living organism, which is strengthened in proselytizing when it is strengthened in any department by contributions from other than its own members.

Such contributions may not be made by the State even in a minor degree without violating the Establishment Clause. It is not the amount of public funds expended; as this case illustrates, it is the use to which public funds are put that is controlling. For the First Amendment does not say that some forms of establishment are allowed; it says that "no law respecting an establishment of religion" shall be made. What may not be done directly may not be done in-directly lest the Establishment Clause become a mockery.[114]

The problem with resting on such literal interpretation is that it provides no answer to those who say that the Constitution says only that Congress shall make no such law and that it does not say that any contribution is the equivalent of establishment. At least it should be noted that the Douglas theory is not self-evident. But it may provide a hint as to where the Kennedy administration derived the notion that the Supreme Court had already decided that federal aid to parochial schools was forbidden by specific Supreme Court pronouncement.

4. *Mr. Justice Goldberg's opinion.*—Mr. Justice Goldberg was the only Justice, other than Mr. Justice Clark, who was able to secure the commitment of another member of the Court: his opinion was joined by Mr. Justice Harlan. Although he, too, con-curred in the opinion of the Court, there were a few matters which he wanted to clarify. His first proposition is one worthy of ap-plause: "These two proscriptions are to be read together, and in light of the single end which they are designed to serve."[115] But if he agreed with a doctrine of neutrality, he objected to the possi-bility of too much neutrality:

[U]ntutored devotion to the concept of neutrality can lead to invoca-tion or approval of results which partake not simply of that noninter-ference and noninvolvement with the religious which the Constitution commands, but of a brooding and pervasive devotion to the secular and a passive, or even active, hostility to the religious. Such results are not only not compelled by the Constitution, but, it seems to me, are prohibited by it.[116]

He, too, was concerned about problems external to the case before the Court. He pointed to the many practices, such as maintenance of military chaplains and religious instruction generally, that would have to be tolerated, but he asserted that the activity in this

---

114 *Id.* at 1575. (Emphasis in original.)

115 *Id.* at 1615. See note 83 *supra*.

116 *Ibid.*

case came clearly within the ban. And, finally, the statement of his own opinion revealed that the opinion of the Court in which he concurred was not the opinion as written by Mr. Justice Clark, but the opinion as rewritten by Mr. Justice Goldberg:

The pervasive religiosity and direct governmental involvement inhering in the prescription of prayer and Bible reading in the public schools, during and as part of the curricular day, involving young impressionable children whose school attendance is statutorily compelled, and utilizing the prestige, power, and influence of school administration, staff, and authority, cannot realistically be termed simple accommodation, and must fall within the interdiction of the First Amendment. I find nothing in the opinion of the Court which says more than this.[117]

In the opinion of Justices Goldberg and Harlan it remains for the Court to determine, case by case, when the line is overstepped; and there is no general guiding principle other than the language of the Constitution itself. To paraphrase T. R. Powell, how much neutrality is too much neutrality was beyond the scope of this opinion. It is disingenuous to suggest that this is the position that was taken by Mr. Justice Clark, who was certainly groping for a principled decision, even if he failed to achieve it.

5. *Mr. Justice Stewart's dissent.*—Mr. Justice Stewart's opinion is reminiscent of some TV westerns. For him there is no neutrality. You're either fur religion or agin it; and he's fur it. The religion clauses of the First Amendment "can not accurately be reflected in a sterile metaphor. . . ."[118] "It is . . . a fallacious oversimplification to regard these two provisions as establishing a single constitutional standard of 'separation of church and state,' which can be mechanically applied in every case to delineate the required boundaries between government and religion."[119] Indeed, in a rather shocked and ingenuous tone, he suggested that the purposes of the establishment clause and the purposes of the free-exercise clause may conflict.

The Justice was not so intransigent all the way through his opinion, however. He conceded that the free-exercise clause was

[117] *Id.* at 1616.   [118] *Id.* at 1617.   [119] *Ibid.*

included in the Fourteenth and, somewhat more reluctantly, conceded that the establishment clause was also applicable to the states. But in his view the problem is not how to protect the minorities from imposition by the majority, but rather how to allow the majority to avoid being imposed on by the minority. To preclude the religious ceremonies in the schools is to establish secularism by "the ritualistic invocation of the nonconstitutional phrase 'separation of church and state.' "[120] His essential argument is somewhat difficult to comprehend, for it turned on the proposition that religious ceremonies, so long as they do not constitute religious instruction, are permissible under the establishment clause. So long as the state itself does not designate "a particular religious book and a denominational prayer," but leaves the choice to the members of the school community, no constitutional infringement has occurred.[121] He was not prepared, on the records presented to him, to decide whether the government or the governed, in fact, chose the texts to be read and the prayers to be recited. So long as local variations are permitted, the protests must fail.

Finally, he suggested that the entire issue should have turned on the existence of compulsion imposed on the dissenters, a subject on which both records were barren of evidence.[122] Compulsion or coercion might be subtle, but it would have to be demonstrable to satisfy Mr. Justice Stewart.

Like his brethren who wrote in this case, Mr. Justice Stewart concludes with a peroration, skeptical, if not agnostic, in tone:

What our Constitution indispensably protects is the freedom of each of us, be he Jew or Agnostic, Christian or Atheist, Buddhist or Freethinker, to believe or disbelieve, to worship or not worship, to pray or keep silent, according to his own conscience, uncoerced and unrestrained by government. It is conceivable that these school boards, or even all school boards, might eventually find it impossible to administer a system of religious exercises during school hours in such a way as to meet this constitutional standard—in such a way as completely to free from any kind of official coercion those who do not

[120] *Id.* at 1619.   [121] *Id.* at 1620.   [122] *Id.* at 1620–22.

affirmatively want to participate. But I think we must not assume that school boards so lack the qualities of inventiveness and good will as to make impossible the achievement of that goal.[123]

III. FURTHER EVALUATION

Despite the wide-eyed surprise with which *Engel v. Vitale* was greeted by its detractors, serious students of the subject hardly found it startling. Indeed, many of them, not classifiable even by the Court's most vehement critics as "secularists," not only anticipated the result but seemed to think it the proper one. Thus, in 1953, Professor Wilber Katz wrote:

As to public schools, the problem of neutrality may be stated as a problem of keeping the schools secular (*i.e.*, ruling out any attempt to inculcate religious belief) and yet avoiding inculcation of secularism (*i.e.*, a philosophy of life which leaves no place for religion). Such neutrality is not easy to achieve.

Except in the released time and flag salute cases, the Supreme Court has not yet been required to decide questions concerning public school programs. The problem of Bible reading was recently before the Court, but the case was dismissed without a decision. *Devotional exercises in public schools, however simple and nonsectarian, are difficult to reconcile with a rule of neutrality.* Such exercises present a problem quite different from that presented by incidental inclusion of religious material in literary and social studies. Occasionally, advocates of strict church-state separation demand careful exclusion of all references to religion. Handling of such material on a basis of neutrality may not always be easy, but consistently to exclude it is to abandon neutrality at the outset.[124]

The result in the *Schempp* case came as even less of a surprise. Once *Engel* had been decided, only a surrender to the political power of the churches similar to that made in *Zorach* could have caused the Court to decide the *Schempp* case otherwise.[125] The Presbyterian Church recognized this and, indeed, even suggested

---

[123] *Id.* at 1622.

[124] Katz, *Freedom of Religion and State Neutrality*, 20 U. CHI. L. REV. 426, 438 (1953). (Emphasis added.) *Cf.* KAUPER, CIVIL LIBERTIES AND THE CONSTITUTION 39–41 (1962) ; Sutherland, *Due Process and Disestablishment*, 62 HARV. L. REV. 1306, 1338–39 (1949).

[125] See Kurland, *supra* note 81, at 32.

that the Court ban Bible-reading.[126] The National Council of Churches of Christ anticipated the result and applauded it.[127] Even the Jesuits foresaw it, however much they deplored it.[128] Most students of the subject clearly expected the result the Court reached.[129]

Moreover, however novel the issues of school prayer and Bible-reading may have been for the Supreme Court, they have been the subject of litigation in state courts for many years.[130] And if it is true that the majority of the state courts—prior to the Supreme Court's application of the religion clauses to the states—have sustained the validity of such activities, that has been largely due to the fact that "Protestantism has been the dominant religious force in helping to shape the pattern of American life and the content of American culture."[131] The state court decisions have not been unanimous, however. Illinois, for example, long ago banned devotional exercises in its public schools, for reasons very much like those suggested in *Engel* and *Schempp*, without the resultant destruction of religious life that the present critics of the Court so dolefully predict. And it is not insignificant that the successful attack in Illinois was made by Catholic interests, not by the "secular" evildoers that the Catholic hierarchy

[126] See Time, May 31, 1963, p. 58.

[127] See Washington Post, May 25, 1963, p. 1, col. 4; *cf.* 30 CHRISTIAN CENTURY 820 (1963).

[128] See N.Y. Times, May 25, 1963, p. 28, col. 2; *cf.* Rodes, *The Passing of Nonsectarianism*, 38 NOTRE DAME LAW 115 (1963).

[129] See Katz, *Religion in the Public Schools*, Chicago Sun-Times, June 16, 1963, § 2, p. 1.

[130] The cases are collected in Harrison, *The Bible, the Constitution and Public Education*, 29 TENN. L. REV. 363, 380–90 (1962).

[131] KAUPER, *op. cit. supra* note 124, at 4. "The public school system as it first developed and as it has continued in some parts of the country to this day was essentially a Protestant school system, and it is not surprising that despite the Protestant emphasis on separation of church and state, the reading of the King James version of the Bible as a devotional exercise was not uncommonly an accepted part of the public school program. And the idea that no public funds should go to support competing schools, notably parochial or religious schools, has revealed another distinctive aspect of Protestant thinking." *Id.* at 4–5.

singled out for criticism in its comments on the prayer decisions.[132] In *Ring v. Board of Education*,[133] Catholic parents secured an order of mandamus forbidding the reading of the King James Bible, the singing of hymns, and recital of the Lord's Prayer in the public schools. The Illinois courts held these devotional activities invalid despite the fact that the school had excused from compliance the Catholic children whose parents brought the suit.

> The exclusion of a pupil from this part of the school exercises in which the rest of the school joins, separates him from his fellows, puts him in a class by himself, deprives him of his equality with the other pupils, subjects him to a religious stigma and places him at a disadvantage in the school, which the law never contemplated. All this is because of his religious belief. If the instruction or exercise is such that certain of the pupils must be excused from it because it is hostile to their or their parents' religious beliefs, then such instruction or exercise is sectarian and forbidden by the constitution.[134]

In disposing of the school prayer cases, the Court was faced with the ordinary problems of the legal process;[135] evolution, not revolution, was the effect of its judgments.

To say that the results of the *Engel* and *Schempp* decisions were not surprising, however, is not to say that they answered all the problems that were presented. One neglected problem was the issue of standing to sue, ignored or befogged by the opinions in these cases. In none of the three cases was the issue of standing raised in the Supreme Court. In *Engel* the Court maintained a discreet silence on the subject.[136] In *Schempp* the several Justices who mentioned it relegated it to footnote consideration.

---

[132] See notes 3 and 12 *supra.*

[133] 245 Ill. 334, 92 N.E. 251 (1910). See also Herold v. Parish Board of School Directors, 136 La. 1034, 68 So. 116 (1915) ; Weiss v. District Board, 76 Wis. 177, 44 N.W. 967 (1890) ; Freeman v. Scheve, 65 Neb. 853, 91 N.W. 846 (1902) ; Finger v. Weedman, 55 S.D. 343, 226 N.W. 348 (1929).

[134] 245 Ill. at 351, 92 N.E. at 256.

[135] See LEVI, INTRODUCTION TO LEGAL REASONING (1st Phoenix ed. 1961).

[136] See Kurland, *supra* note 81, at 19.

Neither action is surprising in light of the history of the subject in the Court.

The question of proper standing in the establishment cases has wound its way over a tortuous path. In *McCollum,* the first re-leased-time case, the right of the mother of a school child to maintain the suit was challenged. Mr. Justice Black, for the majority, quickly disposed of the issue: "A second ground for the motion to dismiss is that the appellant lacks standing to maintain the action, a ground which is also without merit. *Coleman v. Miller,* 307 U.S. 433, 443, 445, 464."[137] The reference to *Miller* hardly clarifies the basis for the holding. At the first place cited, *Miller* stated: "[W]here the claim of a complainant that a state officer be restrained from enforcing a state statute because of constitutional invalidity is sustained by the state court, the statute enables the state officer to seek a reversal by this Court of that decision."[138] Of course, no such issue was presented by *McCollum.* On the second dictum page referred to, the Hughes opinion for the Court in *Miller* asserted: "[T]he Court has sustained the more immediate and substantial right of a resident taxpayer to invoke the interposition of a court of equity to enjoin an illegal use of moneys by a municipal corporation."[139] But, as Mr. Justice Jackson asserted in his concurring opinion, there was no showing of monetary expenditure in *McCollum.* The third reference was to Mr. Justice Frankfurter's opinion, in which Justices Roberts, Black, and Douglas joined. But this provides no greater assistance. The principle there stated was: "No matter how seriously infringement of the Constitution may be called into question, this is not the tribunal for its challenge except by those who have some specialized interest of their own to vindicate, apart from a political concern which belongs to all."[140]

The so-called "pocketbook" rationale was the justification for jurisdiction in *Everson:* "It is true that this Court found a jus-

---

[137] McCollum v. Board of Education, 333 U.S. 203, 206 (1948).

[138] Coleman v. Miller, 307 U.S. 433, 443 (1939).

[139] *Id.* at 445.

[140] *Id.* at 464.

ticiable controversy in *Everson*. . . . But Everson showed a measur-
able appropriation or disbursement of school-district funds occasioned solely by the activities complained of."[141] In *Doremus*, an
appeal from a state-court judgment sustaining Bible-reading in
New Jersey public schools, the Court disclaimed jurisdiction on
the ground that the pupil whose parent sued had been graduated
and the taxpayer could not show any expenditure for the activity
in question on which to predicate his standing to sue. The language of the majority opinion suggested that even had the pupil
not been graduated there would still be no standing:

In support of the parent-and-school-child relationship . . . . there is
no assertion that she was injured or even offended [by the Bible
reading] . . . or that she was compelled to accept, approve or confess
agreement with any dogma or creed or even to listen when the Scrip-
tures were read.[142]

When the released-time program was again in question in
Zorach, the Court acknowledged an absence of "expenditure of
public funds"[143] but sustained jurisdiction and distinguished
Doremus because the petitioners were "parents of children currently attending schools subject to the released-time program."[144]
Doremus still lived when the Court sustained jurisdiction in 1961
in the Maryland Sunday closing-law case on the ground that
appellants "concededly have suffered direct economic injury."[145]
This economic interest was suggested as the basis for distinguishing the rule in *Doremus*, "where complainants failed to show
direct and particular economic detriment."[146]

In *Engel*, all the defects of allegation noted by the Court in
Doremus were avoided, but there is no indication in either
Schempp or *Murray* of any satisfaction of the *Doremus* require-

141 Doremus v. Board of Education, 342 U.S. 429, 434 (1952).

142 *Id*. at 432.

143 Zorach v. Clauson, 343 U.S. 306, 308–9 (1952).

144 *Id*. at 309, n.4.

145 McGowan v. Maryland, 366 U.S. 420, 430 (1961).

146 *Id*. at 430, n.8.

ments. The result is that the problem is disposed of by a tour de force. The Court's opinion in *Schempp* acknowledges the requirement of standing. "It goes without saying," the Court declared, "that the laws and practices involved here can be challenged only by persons having standing to complain."[147] The plaintiffs are then said to satisfy this requirement because they "are school children and their parents, who are directly affected by the laws and practices against which their complaints are directed."[148] *Doremus* is distinguished not in terms of the standard it purported to utilize but in terms of its facts. The school child had graduated and the parties failed to establish standing as taxpayers. This seems to suggest that either of the two qualifications would suffice. More realistically, it is to be expected that it is school attendance that really qualifies a person to sue and that taxpaying status by itself will not suffice.

In the footnote relevant to this subject, Mr. Justice Brennan's opinion puts forth two reasons—in addition to the suggestion that it is a matter of judicial discretion—for sustaining the standing of the plaintiffs in these cases:

First, the parent is surely the person most directly and immediately concerned about and affected by the challenged establishment, and to deny him standing either in his own right or on behalf of his child might effectively foreclose judicial inquiry into serious breaches of the prohibitions of the First Amendment—even though no special monetary injury could be shown. . . . Kurland, The Regents' Prayer Case: "Full of Sound and Fury, Signifying . . . ," 1962 Supreme Court Review 1, 22. Second, the complaint in every case thus far challenging an establishment has set forth at least a colorable claim of infringement of free exercise. When the complaint includes both claims, and neither is frivolous, it would surely be over-technical to say that a parent who does not detail the monetary cost of the exercises to him may ask the court to pass only upon the free-exercise claim, however logically the two may be related.[149]

The difficulty here, as elsewhere in these opinions, continues to derive from the notion that the two clauses detail separate stand-

[147] 83 Sup. Ct. at 1572, n.9.

[148] *Ibid.*   [149] *Id.* at 1594–95, n.30.

ards rather than a single one. It is this same difficulty that caused
the Court, both in *Engel* and *Schempp*, to handle the problem of
coercion so gingerly. Certainly the coercive element is at the
heart of the Brennan opinion, just as it is of the Stewart opinion.
However much it has been denied or ignored, it has also certainly
been an important element in each of the establishment clause cases
that have come before the Court.[150] The difference between the
standing issue and the coercion issue that derives from these cases,
however, is that the Court would seem to have dispensed with the
pocketbook test for standing in cases arising under either of the
religion clauses. It says that it has dispensed with the necessity
for coercion under the establishment clause, but it is not very clear
that it means what it says.

IV. CONCLUSION

This, and only this, is certainly to be derived from the *Engel* and
Schempp cases. The states may not prescribe the conduct of religious ceremonies in their public schools. To read more into the
opinions, as the Court's detractors attempt to do, to see the opinions as destructive of religious life in the United States, is so
patently absurd as to deserve to be ignored. The difficulty is that,
as Hitler so adequately demonstrated, the "big lie" has real utility
as a political technique. And so, if it is said often enough that
the Court is seeking, through its judicial opinions, to destroy religion or establish the "religion of secularism," the technique may
be used to sap the Court of its strength. For it has been clear at
least since Tocqueville, that the Court's power is totally dependent upon the esteem in which it is held by the public. The
sole defense that the Court has against such powers as would
destroy it is the power of the principled decision: a demonstration that the results it reaches in these and other cases are not
dependent on the whim of the majority but rather on the even-
handed application of a principle to the facts and parties before it.
Mr. Justice Clark's opinion took a step toward the development of
such a principle for application in the religion-clauses cases. The

[150] See Kurland, *supra* note 81, at 29.

principle was obfuscated, however, probably because of the difficulty of stating it and because of the necessity for commanding a majority of the Court to join it.

That *Schempp* does not stand for any principle but the narrow holding that was suggested at the outset of this section is amply demonstrated by the decision handed down the same day in *Sherbert v. Verner*,[151] where the Court sustained the right of a Seventh Day Adventist to secure unemployment compensation despite her unwillingness to do Saturday work that those who were not of her faith would be required to do or forfeit their rights to unemployment compensation. It is, perhaps, more clearly demonstrated by the readiness of those who wrote concurring opinions to join in the Court's opinion as well. For no principle proffered by Mr. Justice Clark is reconcilable with the propositions put forth by Justices Brennan, Goldberg, and Douglas in their separate opinions.[152] The encouraging fact is that the Court is at last searching for an appropriate rationale for the religion clauses. One should not ask that it run before it walks.

[151] 83 Sup. Ct. 1790 (1963).

[152] Certainly that perspicacious student of the Court, Anthony Lewis, must have had his tongue in his cheek when he asserted that "the near unanimity of the Court was impressive." Lewis, *Public Mood Plays Big Role in Court Rulings*, N.Y. Times, June 23, 1963, § 4, p. 4., col. 1.